GCSE Drama for OCR

David Cross • Christopher Reynolds

Heinemann

Published by Heinemann Educational Publishers, Halley Court, Jordan Hill, Oxford OX2 8EJ
A division of Reed Educational and Professional Publishing Ltd

OXFORD MELBOURNE AUCKLAND
JOHANNESBURG BLANTYRE GABORONE
IBADAN PORTSMOUTH (NH) USA CHICAGO

First published 2002

06 05 04 03 02
10 9 8 7 6 5 4 3 2 1

ISBN 0 435 18610 8

Designed and produced by Gecko Ltd, Bicester, Oxon
Original illustrations © Heinemann Educational Publishers 2002
Illustrations by DTP – Gecko; Alice Englander; Georgina McBain; Martin Ursell
Printed and bound in the U.K. by Bath Colourbooks Ltd

Acknowledgements
The authors gratefully acknowledge the contribution of Clare Hoyland to the devising of the proformas in Section C. They would also like to thank: Matthew Spencer and Compound Productions Limited www.compoundproductionslimited.co.uk; Trading Faces www.tradingfaces.demon.co.uk; and Rod Morris.

The publishers gratefully acknowledge the following for permission to reproduce copyright material. Every effort has been made to trace copyright holders, but in some cases has proved impossible. The publishers would be happy to hear from any copyright holder that has not been acknowledged.

Extract from *A Man for All Seasons* by Robert Bolt, published by Heinemann. Reprinted with permission; Extract from *The Trojan Women* by Euripides, adapted by Jean Paul Sartre, English Version by Ronald Duncan (Hamish Hamilton 1967) Copyright © 1965 Editions Gallimard. English Version Copyright © 1967, Ronald Duncan. Reprinted by permission of Penguin UK Limited

The Romeo and Juliet Trial (page 123) has been adapted from an article entitled 'Some Experiences with Shakespeare' by Simon Taylor which first appeared in '2D Drama and Dance' magazine, 1984, vol. 3, no. 3. The plague poem (page 138) was written by Linda Davies and Linda Warrilow.

The publishers would like to thank the following for permission to reproduce photographs on the pages noted:

Keith Thomson (3 characters, p10; *Animal Farm*, p16; *Tropical Treats*, p21; *Happy End*, p23; naturalistic set, p40; pantomime, p72; *Trojan Women*, p134); Trading Faces/Rod Morris (woman in coffin, p12; three masks, p42); Donald Cooper (In-the-round staging, p26; proscenium staging, p27; *Look Back in Anger*, p38); Wayland Picture Library (domestic scene, p32); William Timbers/Matthew Spencer/Compound Production Ltd (improviser, p33); Mary Evans Picture Library (Victorian Christmas, p66; Russian poster, p77; evacuees, p81); Hannah Burton (Scrooge props, p67; *Macbeth* props, p112; *Macbeth* museum, p132); Hulton (underground, p81; firefighters, p81); Impact (council estates; graffiti door, p106); Arena Images/Hanya Chlala (backstage, p129)

Contents

Dedications

David Cross
dedicates this book
to the memory of his father
Alfred Rees Cross

Christopher Reynolds
dedicates this book
to his wife
Maureen
with thanks for her
constant help and support

Introduction

The aim of this book is to help you get better marks for your GCSE Drama.

The book is divided into three sections.

Section A

In Section A, each one of the areas of study is explored. Its meaning is defined, and activities are suggested that might help you with your understanding. There are tips on things the examiner will be looking for, and a section for those of you who work really fast and want to get your teeth into more!

Section B

In Section B, there are examples you can work through with your teacher for each of the units. This will help you complete your coursework, and will prepare you for both the written paper and the practical examination.

Section C

In Section C you will find practical tips and suggestions about each part of the examination.

There will be ideas about:

- how to record what you do for your portfolios
- ways of answering questions in the written paper
- preparing for the practical examination
- undertaking the practical examination.

We hope that you enjoy using this book and wish you much success as you study GCSE Drama.

David Cross
Christopher Reynolds

What you have to study in the OCR Drama course is set out in the specification. Your teacher will have a copy of this, but this section of the book will explain it for you. The specification describes what you have to know, what you have to do and how you will be assessed. There are seven areas of study. They cover what you have to know, and they are explained in this section.

The approaches

There are four approaches that cover the different ways you will be working:

Deviser

This refers to the creation of drama, whether improvised or in script form. You can create the work, or it can be work created by another person. It includes work created by playwrights and published as plays.

The specification requires two things of you. First, that you are able to create a script yourself using the appropriate areas of study. Secondly, that you have some understanding of how playwrights have created a script, and what skills they have used.

So, for example, when you are working on structure, shaping and plot – area of study (AoS) 2 – you will be thinking about how you will structure and shape your own work, and will also look at how a playwright has structured and shaped a play and why they have done it that way. This applies to any of the areas of study that you might use as part of learning about devising.

Designer

In the past, candidates studying drama looked at things like make-up or costume design as separate elements. This is not the approach of the OCR specification. Design is seen as something that covers all aspects of a piece of drama. When an idea is used to devise drama, there will be different possibilities about how it will be presented, how its message will be put across, or what sort of experience the audience will have. The elements of design will need to be considered, not separately but as a whole, creating an overall design concept for the drama/text. So aspects of set design, costume design, lighting design, make-up, sound design, properties and furniture will all be part of the process of creating a piece of drama.

The specification is based on the idea that each area of design is linked and relies on each other, and so should be considered together, not in isolation. The specification requires each candidate to experience and develop understanding of design. Each area of design may have its own contribution to make, or may not be needed, depending upon the style of the drama.

Director

Once ideas have begun to develop and the drama is under way, the work needs to be guided towards the conclusion of a performance or presentation. This process of guiding the development is called 'directing' in the specification. It means you take ideas and help them to become structured, workable and more effective. It does not mean bossing everyone else around, because the good director will listen to the ideas of others and will use them. Sometimes direction will take place as a combined activity, with several of you taking on the role jointly.

Two key elements are: reviewing what has gone on so far, and making decisions to improve the drama. In this book we use the terms **edit**, **adapt** and **add** to provide a guide to the process of reviewing your work.

Performer

This approach probably seems the most obvious. It relates to the 'doing' of the drama, and the concept of communicating the drama to an audience. It is not just about acting, though – the specification makes it clear that as well as communicating through role and character, communicating through symbol should also be considered under this heading.

Integration of the approaches

The four approaches should be understood separately, but as the course progresses you should use them together. So, if you are working in a group, you may begin in the role of deviser, and then switch to designer, followed by director, back to deviser, then to director again, and then performer. The roles will interlink so that effective drama is created. The specification requires you to develop skills and understanding in using all of the approaches in an integrated way.

Area of study 1 – Character and context

What does the specification say?

Area of study 1	Character and context	
Minimum requirement	*Both must be studied*	
Definition	**Character**: a role created by an actor or writer as part of a presentation, which will be exemplified by external physical features and internal motivation. They may be defined by, for example, their status, class, beliefs, personality, history, job and attitudes. **Context**: the situation or circumstances in which a piece of drama is set or devised, which may have historical, cultural or social influences.	
Examples	The content and influences on a piece of drama, whether devised or scripted; the intention of a playwright in devising a piece of drama; what must be considered by director, actor and designer in preparing to present drama. Areas might include some of the following: Stanislavski's system of character building; representational, Brechtian approach; stereotyping; stock characters.	

What does it mean?

There are two terms here. You need to know what both mean. One is **character**; the other is **context**.

Character

This will probably be quite easy for you to understand. We often talk about other people by saying things like 'She's a funny character...' or 'Look out, he's a tough character...'

Usually what we mean is that we recognise some features of the person. These features may relate to how they look or how they sound. They may relate to the way they laugh or the way they speak. Perhaps it is the way they walk or the way they behave. Are they funny or sad, jolly or grumpy?

> 1 On your own, choose someone you think other students in your class might know. Choose an adult, perhaps a teacher or someone else who works in the school, or perhaps a television or film star. Do not choose another student.
>
> 2 Make a list of things you might recognise them by. Take just five minutes to do this. When told to by your teacher, share your list with another person and see if you can guess who you each have chosen.

Sometimes the features of another person may have something to do with what they do or their position in society. It might be that they have power, or that they have none. They might be a criminal, or very kind.

3 In small groups, get one person to suggest a person that you might all know. Make a list of the features by which you might recognise them. One person should act as note-taker. Have two columns to your list: one for personal things like happy, kind etc.; the other for things to do with their position in society. Do this for a second example, picking someone different.

The things you have listed are some of the things that might define the person.

In a play, the actor will be representing or creating a role. To be successful, the role must come to life, must have meaning. The sorts of things on your lists are the things that an actor or director may have to understand and use in developing the role.

The specification gives a list of things that might define the role.

Status	What is their power or position in society?
Class	Are they poor or well-off, working or middle class?
Beliefs	Are there things they feel strongly about that drive them?
Personality	What are the individual things about the person?
History	What is their background, how they grew up, what makes them what they are?
Job	What do they do, what is their occupation?
Attitudes	How do they see life or other people, or themselves?

4 Turn to page 51. Look at scenario A. In small groups, build up the profile for the character of the burglar. Use the list above to help you. You will have to use the information provided to build up your character. Some of it is obvious, other things may provide clues, and for some things there will be no information at all.

Sometimes characters are described as 'flat' or 'one-dimensional'. This means that they have no depth, that an audience, in seeing them, is not able to discover much about them, or understand why they are behaving in the way they are. Just the obvious characteristics are on show.

5 One of your group stands in the centre of the group. This person represents the burglar. One at a time, **mould** this person to demonstrate a characteristic of the burglar that could be represented visually. Imagine the person is a statue and you are sculpting it.

It is not always wrong to have simple characters. We can recognise certain sorts of people by set characteristics, and this can be an easy way to communicate meaning to an audience, or to create comedy or fear. There are traditional expectations of certain sorts of characters.

6 Read scenario B on page 51. What are the characteristics of the role of the Head? Would they be different if the Head were old or young? Would they be different if the Head were a man or a woman? How would the Head be dressed? What would the voice sound like?

In pairs, try out the scene described, from the pupil coming out of the classroom and walking along the corridor.

Try it out with different outcomes. Focus on how the Head speaks and behaves. After each run through, talk about what made a difference, and how you might change the scene by using different voices and showing a different character. How would you show the scene if the Head was mean and nasty, or kind and understanding?

Characters such as the Headteacher of a school often create in our minds a set of images, a set of characteristics that give the idea of 'Headteacher'. This is often called a **stereotype**.

7 Can you think of any other stereotypes? Use a still image and give the image a caption or title, such as 'the worried parent' or 'the bad-tempered teenager'.

Some plays use stereotypes deliberately, almost as a form of shorthand, a quick way to give information to the audience. The best examples are television soaps such as *EastEnders* or *Coronation Street*, where the characters are instantly recognisable because of the way they behave. Some characters may remind us of people we know. When stereotypes are used in this way they can become what is called 'stock characters', representing a type or occupation rather than an individual: the barman or barmaid; the flighty young girl or the drunken young man; the layabout who is always looking for a way to make easy money; the elderly couple; the nagging wife or husband, and so on.

8 Look at the photograph above. What sort of characteristics would you want to develop from the evidence in the photo? Be inspired by the photo and develop your own character. Be interviewed by someone else about your life as the character.

There are other ways in which character might be used.

In the medieval play *Everyman*, the characters all represent something. For example, the character named Everyman represents all living people, and the character named Good Deeds represents all the good things Everyman has done in his life. Even things that happen are represented by a character in the play. An example of this is Death, who comes to collect the body of the person who is to die. This is an idea that has appeared in lots of plays, especially with characters like Death.

9 Can you think of any characters in plays or films that represent an idea or thing rather than a real person?

So, building up a character requires you to take lots of things into consideration. The specification expects you to know how to do that, to select what is best to make an effective character, and what are the most important things.

Context

The specification defines context as 'the situation or circumstances in which a piece of drama is set or devised, which may have historical, cultural or social influences'.

Probably the best way to understand this is to think of five questions.

What?

This is a description of the action: what is actually happening.
Is there a narrative? Is it a representation?

Who?

Who are the characters concerned? What is their background, what makes them what they are? Have they families or friends? How are they linked to other characters?

Why?

What is the reason for what is happening? Is it an action, such as the burglary in scenario A? Is it simply telling a story, an entertainment? Or is there a message that the writer wants to transmit? Are the audience to be educated or to experience a spectacle? Is it a snapshot of real life?

Where?

What is the location of the action? The Greeks in writing their plays restricted the locations to ones that could be represented in real life, where little imagination was needed. In Shakespeare's plays we are often transported to other countries, and even to imaginary islands where magic occurs. In many modern plays, for example those by Alan Ayckbourn, plays are set in ordinary people's living rooms.

When?

This can refer not only to simple time issues such as the time of day, but also to time in history. The time in history will bring with it different social conditions, different expectations, different customs, different ways of looking at things.

These five ways of looking at drama are used quite a lot in section B.

10 Look at scenarios A and B on page 51. Devise a short scene for one of them, but setting it a hundred years ago. What would change? How would the characters speak? How would they be dressed? What else might change?

Sometimes cultural difference caused by time or by cultural backgrounds can have a very big impact. For example, in our society the role of women has changed considerably over the last hundred years, and in some societies the roles for men and women are very clearly defined.

11 Prepare a short scene using scenario D on page 52. Prepare two versions: one set in the present, the other set in a time when women did not have the vote and were treated very much as the servants of men.

Remember that there are some cultures where the role of women is still very subservient to that of men.

In some plays, it is the context that is more important than the characters. This might be the case where the focus is the horrors of war, or perhaps poverty and poor living conditions. In such drama it might be that the characters are used almost as part of the stage picture rather than as fully developed characters in their own right.

12 Look at the photograph above. If this was the context for a drama, what do you think might be the context? What characters might you choose to be part of such a drama? Develop a series of still images (sometimes called freeze-frame pictures) where the context is the most important thing. Repeat this, treating the characters as more important. How does the change of focus affect what you do?

What are the examiners looking for?

When you are devising, the examiners will expect to see that you understand and have thought about character and context. They will want to see that you have a definite idea in your mind when developing a **character**, that you have thought about what sort of character it is, and what will help the character to communicate to the audience. Aspects of design could be very important here. What costume would they wear, and how might this add to the impact of the character? Is make-up appropriate or necessary? And if so, what sort of design might be needed? For **context**, they will expect you to have thought out the implications of where and when a play is set, and to think about this in your devising, as well. You need to understand what impact the setting may have on how characters behave and speak.

Tasks and challenges

1 Write, or devise verbally with others, the outline for the next scene for scenario A on page 51. What will we learn about the two characters in the next scene? How will an audience learn more about the two characters just by looking and listening?

2 Choose a character from one of the plays you are studying. Using the checklist given on page 9, prepare a profile for the character as if you were going to play the role. Devise a short scene where your character meets one or more of the other characters in the play you are studying.

3 What design issues might there be in either or both of the above? How could you make your scene more effective through the use of lighting, costume and make-up?

TOP TIPS

Character and context go together well because they have an effect on each other. Top candidates will be able to integrate their thinking about them so that the examiner can see that you know that for meaning to be communicated about a character, there has to be an understanding of the situation in which the character is placed.

Use the list on page 9 when thinking about developing character, or assessing a character in a play.

Explain the **function** of the character. Is it to be a way of helping the story along; simply a means of reflecting life; or is it a way of telling the audience something?

Examiners will notice if you have not only thought out the characteristics of a role and the context that might affect the character, but also have a clear idea of the purpose and function of the character.

In coursework in Unit 2 examiners will be looking to see whether you use things you learnt as part of your coursework in Unit 1. You can show this by referring to the plays you studied and the characters and contexts you explored. Then show how this has helped or influenced you in your thinking about the work you are doing for Unit 2.

Want to know more? Research and extras

- Find out about *commedia dell'arte* and its stock characters. Look at the bibliography at the end of this book if you need help in finding a source.

- If you would like to know more about *Everyman*, look at scenario C on page 52, and investigate medieval theatre. Constance Cox has written a short modern adaptation.

- Stanislavski was a practitioner who did a lot of work on the development of a character. He wrote a book called *Creating a Character*. See if you can find out about his major points in creating a role.

- Find out about the Greek unities of time, place and action.

Area of study 2 – Structure, shaping and plot

What does the specification say?

Area of study 2	Structure, shaping and plot	
Minimum requirement	*More than one approach must be applied to the creation of a drama*	
Definition	**Structure** and **shaping**: whole constructed unit; the way a piece of drama is put together; the connections between a series of sections; a framework; a definite or proper arrangement of a piece of drama work; a form which has some meaning; the total effect. **Plot**: the outline of a literary work; the structure of the action of the play. The character responds to the situation and other characters, who in turn respond.	
Examples	Play form, the 'well-made play', unities of time and place, epic theatre, mixed media presentations, conventions of plot and time, sketches and scripts, devices for closure. Models exist which can be used for dramatic planning. Candidates should be introduced to some of these to assess their strengths and the possibilities they offer to the candidates' own work. For example: Aristotelian model (exposition, rising action, climax, dénouement); peripetia (twist in the plot); obligatory moments (moments the audience anticipate and feel cheated if they do not get); stream of consciousness (no structure except to follow the flow); montage; vignettes and collage; varying chronological order; allegory and satire; irony and metaphor.	

What does it mean?

Many plays are divided up in some way. The most common division is into Scenes and Acts. A 'change of scene' usually means a new idea is introduced, the location changes, or a new character is presented. In what is often called the **well-made play**, the sequence of the structure is: characters are introduced; the action develops; it rises to a climax; then issues are resolved. The playwright does this to try and make sure that what they write will make sense when it is performed. You must have the same thoughts, so that the drama work produced is not haphazard, or shaped by accident.

There are three key words.

structure **shaping** **plot**	

They are all interconnected. The specification explains that **structure** is the framework of the drama, the way sections are put together. If there is no formal framework, structure refers to the description of the way the drama will proceed and progress.

Shaping is taking it one step further, and has a link with meaning. Shaping is the way the drama is constructed within the framework (structure) to give the meaning or effect intended by the creator of the drama. It may refer to small sections, even a few lines or words, an entrance or exit, or a crucial event and when it occurs.

Plot is used to describe what happens, and when. It is the story that is to be told and how the telling of it is to be organised.

1 Have a look at scenario E on page 53.

Make a copy of the grid below and fill it in, or use it as a guide for discussion with others in your group.

Structure	Brief note of content
Scene 1	
Scene 2	
Scene 3	
Scene 4	

2 What parts of the scenario might you want to consider in shaping the material?

The first four rows of the grid below describe the **Aristotlean model** for a drama. Copy the grid and write down any examples of the items in the left-hand column that you can find in scenario E.

Exposition Giving the necessary information.	
Rising action The things that happen build up in pace and perhaps excitement.	
Climax Matters come to a head – there is a moment of catharsis or emotional release.	
Dénouement Everything is explained.	
Peripetia A twist in the plot.	
Obligatory moments Those moments in the action where the audience expect something to happen and feel cheated if it doesn't.	

The specification gives some other examples of influences on structure, shaping and plot, as outlined on pages 16–17. Use what you learn to help you with the tasks on page 18.

Stream of consciousness

In this style of writing there is no structure except to follow the flow.

The 'flow' may be a series of ideas and almost random episodes. This may be used in improvisation work when wanting to explore an idea or situation, and where the participants want to see where things might lead. For presentation purposes there might need to be a more formal structure, although some theatre companies follow a very flexible pattern of outcomes. Sometimes a play has a variety of endings: which one is used depends on circumstances earlier in the play, or even the intervention of the audience in a role, such as a jury coming to a verdict that is not known in advance.

Montage

A series or collection of stage pictures, often used when showing a series of events where the spectacle is as important as the characters, or as the plot, if there is any. Examples might include historical events.

Vignettes and collage

Vignette: a short, evocative episode, which may focus on a character or event.

Collage: a series of illustrations or scenes with a common background, possibly a series of images where what is seen and experienced may be more important than what is heard in dialogue.

Business is business – a scene from Peter Hall's adaptation of *Animal Farm*.

Varying chronological order

In what is known as 'the well-made play', the action progresses in an order following time, as would happen in everyday life. This structure can be varied, however. The most popular variation is that of **flashback**, where the meat of the plot is contained in events that occurred before the starting point of the play. In such drama, the option is open for the beginning to be the ending as well, and the thrust of the play to be about the journey; or there could be a twist where the audience is led to believe that the beginning preceding the flashback will be the ending, but there is actually a further development after returning to the present.

Sometimes flashback, and similar ways of flitting between present and other periods of time, past and future, can be helped along by the use of a narrator.

Allegory and satire

Scenario C on page 52 provides an example of an allegory. An allegory is a story or picture in which the meaning is represented through symbols. In the case of the play *Everyman*, this is achieved through characters playing ideas like 'Good Deeds' and articles such as 'Wealth'. Satire is the use of ridicule, irony or sarcasm to expose foolishness or wrong-doing, or to send up or make fun of an individual. It is often used to make fun of political characters. The play *Animal Farm* by Peter Hall, based on the book by George Orwell, represents both allegory and satire, using ridicule and irony to expose foolishness.

Irony and metaphor

Irony: using language that reflects the opposite of what is actually happening – a form of sarcasm. Dramatic irony refers to the audience knowing something that the characters do not.

Metaphor: using the imagination to describe something by comparing it to something else or saying it is something else. This is usually done to create an effect.

What are the examiners looking for?

In the 'tasks and challenges' section, you are asked a series of questions. If you answer these questions about the work you are doing and can provide evidence to show that you have done this, you will be meeting assessment criteria.

This is also true of the written paper and the practical examination. Many candidates just put down their ideas for a drama without any thought as to how they might be put together and work in practice. Think about how work can be organised to create the effect you want, even with short pieces of improvisation.

Also think about how changing the structure, or using shaping, or amending the plot, might make the drama more successful. Top candidates will be able to:

➤ draw on a range of structures suiting the purpose of the piece

➤ demonstrate they understand shaping by applying it to important moments in a drama

➤ use plot as a shorthand for describing a story, or consciously reject it in favour of something else (see comments on *Waiting for Godot* on page 19).

Tasks and challenges

1 What differences in structure might there be if you were to develop scenario E on page 53 as:

  - a short comedy sketch
  - a play lasting about half an hour
  - a play lasting for a full evening's entertainment
  - a television play.

  Prepare a short improvisation based on scenario E. Supply two contrasting endings. Will your endings change the structure or shaping of the drama? Why?

2 In coursework in Unit 1 you are considering text. Try to discover:

  - the structure chosen by the playwright – and why
  - what shaping in the material has occurred that you, as a director or an actor, want to understand
  - the plot – give a summary
  - if a different structure might have worked.

3 In coursework in Unit 2 you will be creating your own work.

  - What structure will you choose and why?
  - What is the plot?
  - What in the plot will need shaping to ensure the meaning or effect is communicated successfully to an audience?

TOP TIPS

A very useful way to show an examiner you have really thought about this is to refer to scripts you have studied and compare their structure with work you are devising. It is even better if you say *why* you have chosen to use a particular structure or to shape a particular scene by comparing it to something you have seen or studied or done in the past.

The most important thing is to demonstrate that you know what each of the three terms means, and that you use them when looking at existing scripts and devising your own work.

It is also important to recognise that there is no right or wrong way to structure a piece of drama. Audiences today accept all sorts of structures and even a mix of them in a single piece of drama.

Want to know more? Research and extras

- Two famous drama practitioners had their own views on structure:

Stanislavski:
Stanislavski described the structure of a play as being like a turkey that a family is having for dinner. The bird is the whole play, sitting there on the plate. Then the wings and legs are torn off, and the breast cut into big chunks. These are the acts. These pieces are then divided further into scenes, and even further until they are small morsels for the mouth. These are small sections of the play, single lines or even words or gestures. This is described in his book, *An Actor Prepares*.

Brecht:
Bertolt Brecht held very different views to Stanislavski, and his plays, especially if they are described as **epic theatre**, did not have scenes that automatically followed on one from another. They have a series of episodes, which together tell a story, but where each episode can stand alone. His views on the difference between epic theatre and the more traditional structure for a play can be found in many of his books. *Brecht on Theatre* is probably the easiest to find.

- The unities of time, place and action used in Greek theatre provide an interesting insight into one view of structure, introduced by Aristotle, but built upon by European practitioners throughout later centuries. This is explained in more detail in section B on page 96 (Top tip).
- Samuel Beckett's play *Waiting for Godot* has an interesting structure (see scenario F on page 54). Beckett held the view that plot was not important because the focus should not be on what happens, but how it happens. This means that as there is no real development in the story, the symbols and meanings become important. Bear this in mind when looking at area of study 7 on semiotics. Consider how the nature of a play might create a very specific structure.

Area of study 3 – Audience

What does the specification say?

Area of study 3	Audience
Minimum requirement	*Contrasting types of audience must be considered in the study of script, and the preparation and devising of drama*
Definition	Those for whom the performance or outcome is intended.
Examples	This could relate to the intention of the playwright, and the issues that the drama raises. Theatre-in-education and documentary, melodrama and political theatre all have their own intended audience. The work of Stanislavski, Brecht, Grotowski, Ayckbourn and Godber, for example, could be considered in relation to their view of audience. This area will link with areas of study 4 and 6.

What does it mean?

This is probably one of the easiest terms to understand, but one that is often ignored by candidates studying drama, because they take it for granted. The concept of 'audience' cannot really be separated from the intention of the playwright.

The definition given in the specification is straightforward: audience is 'those for whom the performance or outcome is intended'.

For the purpose of preparing for the examination, it is important to have a structured approach. Once creativity is under way, and ideas have begun to form, it is worth asking yourself the questions 'Who is going to see this?' and 'What impact do I want this drama to have on those who see it?'

It is not necessary to have a complicated reason for the impact or effect you want. It is quite acceptable for your intention as playwright to be to entertain the audience or to tell a good story. What is required is for you to have an understanding of some of the different intentions that there could be with regard to audience, and to consider this in your work. Several examples are mentioned, although they are not the only ones.

Simpler issues are also considered under this heading. Such things as an audience being able to:

- see what is going on
- see what is happening
- hear
- be safe.

Theatre-in-education

This form of drama has grown greatly over the years, and you may have experienced performances from visiting theatre companies, often on a subject connected with the health and safety of young people. The subject matter may have been drugs, the prevention of smoking, road safety or the dangers of talking to strangers. Whatever the topic, the purpose is to educate the audience, to make a difference, to change outlooks.

Tropical Treats, a scene from a theatre-in-education drama by the Leicestershire Schools Theatre Company

1 As a group, can you remember where you have seen something that might be considered as theatre-in-education? Did it have an impact? Did it change you or others? If so, why? If not, why not, and what could have been changed so that it did have an impact?

Documentary theatre

This style probably began with some of the social drama of the early 1900s, but its greatest popularity in more recent days has been looking at historical events, significant people from the past and issues of the day that may cause comment or concern. The problem for the playwright is to decide the intention. Is it enough to provide factual information, present it effectively, and leave the audience to make up its own mind, judging the rights and wrongs of what they have seen? Or should the playwright construct the drama in such a way that the audience is confronted with stark opposites? The latter is what happens in the play *Oh What a Lovely War* by Joan Littlewood, where the horrors of war are factually reported to an audience as a backdrop to the cavalier attitude of those in power, casually ordering the deaths of hundreds of thousands while sipping drinks in the comfort of their offices.

The playwright will use authentic press cuttings, perhaps people's speeches, and genuine factual information to develop dialogue and design elements.

> **2** Choose an idea from the history of your town or village, or a character or incident, such as a strike or trade dispute, in national history. Prepare a scenario, decide on the plot and a structure. Then select one important part of the scenario and develop a short scene, shaping it to meet your intention. What is your intention? How do you want your audience to respond to your scene?

Agitprop

This style of theatre developed in Germany and Russia in the late 1920s and 1930s. It was linked with the Workers' Theatre Movement, and it had a very specific intention for its audience. It wanted to move away from traditional play audiences, the rich and comfortable, and to reach the masses of workers. Its intention was to give a more robust and realistic view of life and of social issues. It went out to its audiences, whether they were on the street corner, in the park or in their workplace. It had a very direct approach to the audience so that they felt part of what was happening, and that the actors understood what they were suffering. They took just a few days to prepare drama that had something to say about events that were actually happening.

Political theatre

While agitprop is probably rightly considered as political theatre, there are many examples of political theatre where the audience being targeted is more general. The intention of the playwright is usually to make the audience consider certain events and why they occurred; then to come to a decision as to whether it was right and reasonable. The playwright may push the audience in a certain direction by the way the material is presented. One example of political theatre is Berkoff's *The Sinking of the Belgrano*, based on the sinking of the Argentine battleship during the Falklands war. Berkoff deliberately waited several years before publishing the play, so that the writing of it and the viewing of it would not be influenced by the closeness of the event, and the influence of the nationalism that inevitably arises when a country is at war would be avoided. He wanted his audiences to examine the event in cool detachment.

Bertolt Brecht wrote many plays that are considered to be political theatre, where he examines issues of war, justice and social class.

Practitioners

Several practitioners are mentioned in the specification as examples, and some have been mentioned above.

Konstantin Stanislavski wanted his audience to identify with his characters. He wanted his audiences to see the play as a snapshot of real life. The expression 'the fourth wall' is often used to describe this concept. The audience are placed at the fourth wall of a room, peeping in and seeing what is going on. The actors take no notice of the audience, they do not acknowledge their presence in any way. The drama is devised so that the audience empathises with what is going on – that is, they are able to identify themselves with the characters, feel what they are feeling, cry when they cry.

Bertolt Brecht rejected this viewpoint as being a means of hypnotising the audience, taking away their capacity to think and act, and not allowing them to make up their own minds. Brecht took the view that the audience should view what was happening as a spectator, remaining detached, looking on rather than looking in. He described it as a reporter giving an account – his audience should sympathise but not empathise: understand but not become involved.

More modern-day playwrights such as **Caryl Churchill**, **John Godber** and **Alan Ayckbourn** take a more mixed view, and there may be moments when the audience is addressed directly, so no identification or empathy could happen. But in a later scene there may be a very naturalistic episode.

A scene from Bertolt Brecht's *Happy End*.

3 Look at extract A on page 56. Either using the dialogue, or improvising your own, explore and present the extract. Decide your intention based upon it as:

- a piece of naturalistic drama
- a piece of documentary drama
- a piece of theatre-in-education.

Keep thinking about the impact on the audience, and the intention of the playwright, in this case, you. How will it be different depending on the type of audience? It would be interesting for each group to choose a different way and then show each other the result.

Audience expectations

Whilst the intention of the playwright and what is hoped will be the impact upon the audience is important, it should never be forgotten that audiences themselves will have expectations that may affect the playwright. Sometimes this will cause the playwright to deliberately shock and surprise. Throughout history playwrights have had this effect at certain times in the development of theatre. In the late 1800s and early 1900s audiences had come to expect great spectacles with lots of complicated scenery and special effects. Eventually, an audience watching a Shakespeare play could spend longer watching changes of scenery than watching the play itself!

At times, audiences have been affected so strongly that changes in society have occurred. The death of a prisoner at the end of the Galsworthy play *Justice*, in the early 1900s, caused Winston Churchill, who was then Home Secretary, to change the law on solitary confinement; the play *Love on the Dole* by Gow and Greenwood had such an impact on audiences that it increased pressure for change in the regulations concerning the dole. On television, the Documentary Drama *Cathy Come Home* led to the formation of the charity Shelter.

> **4** It is interesting that such changes came about after watching naturalistic theatre. Brecht said he did not believe an audience could have the capacity for change if watching a play produced using naturalism. What do you think?

What are the examiners looking for?

The examiners will want to see:
- ➤ evidence that you have a clear intention in mind when devising work
- ➤ that you have considered the audience
- ➤ that you know what will be needed to have the impact you want on an audience to achieve the intention.

This will apply in all sections of the examination.
Make sure you refer to audience and intention in any portfolio work and in the examination paper.

Tasks and challenges

- Develop a drama that could be performed in front of younger pupils. Choose one of the following:

  either

  a theatre-in-education piece about the dangers of playing in forbidden places, like on the railway, or in an electricity sub-station

  or

  a documentary piece based on a historical event of local importance.

- Be really brave and develop a piece of agitprop drama to perform in front of your peers. The subject could be to do with school or their social lives, should be hard-hitting and a real issue. Your audience needs to feel that you, as actors, really understand what it is like to be them.

- Examine the script you are studying and decide upon the sort of audience that might see the play performed. Is it the same sort of audience now as when it was first written? Will it stand the test of time and still be performed in 50 years' time? What is the intention of the playwright in the play? Is the audience expected to identify with the characters?

- What are the issues of health and safety for an audience? What does a house manager have to consider for the safety of both performers and audience? Consider overcrowding, fire, equipment and any other things that might be a safety issue.

- How do you meet the needs of sight- and/or hearing-impaired members of an audience?

TOP TIPS

Get to grips with the views of some of the practitioners, and form your own view about audiences and the intention of playwrights. You can then refer to them when talking or writing about audience and intention when looking at scripts and devising your own work.

Never refer to a style of doing drama as 'Stanislavskian' or 'Brechtian'. Refer rather to naturalistic, non-naturalistic, episodic, epic theatre, or say your ideas have been influenced by the thinking of the practitioner concerned.

Look carefully at the potential for performance of work, and how to make it accessible to an audience. It is no good spending hours on preparing a piece of drama if the audience fall asleep!

Want to know more? Research and extras

Part of the development of the Workers' Theatre Movement was a collection of theatre groups in Russia in the 1920s, called Blue Blouses because of their blue uniforms. See what you can find out about them and the way they staged their plays, and the response of their audiences. An excerpt from a worker's theatre piece, *Art is a Weapon*, can be seen on the website www.heinemann.co.uk/secondary/drama/.

Area of study 4 – Defining performance space

What does the specification say?

Area of study 4	Defining performance space
Minimum requirements	*Minimum of three venue types/spaces must be considered for the focus of the drama*
Definition	The space to be used for enacting the drama.
Examples	Studio, arena, in-the-round, thrust, promenade, proscenium, traverse staging. The use of buildings – purpose-built theatres; matching intention such as museums, old country houses, factories and mills; street theatre; pub theatre; outdoor theatre. How the space is defined, use of lighting, levels and materials.

What does it mean?

This area of study looks at where the drama will take place. You are expected to know about formal places for presenting drama as well as informal ones. Sometimes the place will be linked with the intention for the drama.

You must make sure you are comfortable with your knowledge of **three** different sorts of spaces or venues. Read through these (pages 26–30), to help you answer the tasks on pages 30–31.

In-the-round and arena

In this staging, the performance space is in the centre of the audience and is surrounded by them on all sides. The shape may be circular or square – indeed any shape. Arena staging originates from the time of the Greeks and Romans, the word 'arena' meaning the space in the centre where activity took place. In-the-round and arena staging is a very popular form of acting space, with new theatres often having the flexibility to be used in this way. There are significant acting, direction and design challenges when the audience is looking at the action from all sides at the same time.

In-the-round staging at The Pit theatre, Barbican, London

Scenery and furniture must never be more than a metre high, and wherever the audience is sitting, each person should almost always be able to see something happening. Entrances and exits need to be carefully set up.

It is a form that theatre practitioner Artaud, in the early 1900s, suggested should be made more use of, even going a step further and suggesting that the action should surround the audience!

Thrust

This staging sticks out into the audience, so that the action is surrounded on three sides. The challenges to designer, performer and director are not quite so great as with in-the-round. This type of staging was very popular in theatres built in the second half of the twentieth century, as it was still fairly close to proscenium staging but allowed greater flexibility.

Promenade

In this type of staging the audience walks around from one set to another, or follows the actors as they move from one location to another.

Proscenium

This staging derives from the 'proscenium arch', which refers to the pillars and crosspiece that make up the division between audience and acting space. Sometimes described as the 'picture frame stage', the name has its origins in Greek theatre, although the meaning was different then. It has been the most common form of staging in theatres in Britain.

Proscenium staging at the Littleton/National Theatre, London

Traverse

This refers to the acting area being between two opposing sets of seating. The Traverse Theatre in Edinburgh is the most well-known theatre in Britain that uses this design.

Theatres

Buildings provided expressly for the performance of drama. Older theatres will probably be in a proscenium arch format; newer ones may be able to add an apron to make the proscenium into a thrust stage; the latest theatres have the option of just about any sort of configuration.

Studio

A purpose-built theatre, but usually much smaller and more intimate, and not normally with a proscenium arch. The space will have rostra and platforms that can be used in a variety of ways. There is the opportunity to be very flexible, as seating will often be 'loose' and so can be arranged in just about any configuration that the fire officer will allow!

Museums, old country houses, factories and mills etc.

There has been a growth in recent years in the use of venues such as these. Sometimes it is part of a marketing exercise; sometimes an attempt to bring to life the story of an event or person in history by performing it in authentic surroundings. Often it will use promenade devices. Murder mystery events have become very popular in hotels and old houses.

Street theatre and pub theatre

This form of acting space is just what it sounds. Strolling players have been around for centuries. The performance takes place in any area big enough for the activity, and with access to an audience. Often it is pure entertainment, perhaps with a focus on particular drama skills such as mime or clowning. There will be times when a story is told, or when issues are addressed, especially if it takes place at the location of some threatened event, such as the closure of a hospital or demolition of a much-loved building.

Theatre in pubs is similar in that it is an attempt to bring drama closer to where people are, rather than taking people away to a theatre. Some companies specialise in this, using upper rooms or the corner of a lounge or bar room.

In both spaces, lighting and scenery are minimal, but sound may play a bigger part. Props also become important, and sometimes there is a lot of attention to costume and make-up.

Outdoor theatre

There are a number of sites around the country that regularly feature outdoor theatre. It is relatively easy to find a production of a Shakespeare play in the grounds of a country house or castle. Some country parks set up stages especially for such performances, and in these instances they are very much like the traditional theatre but without walls and a roof. Others make use of the natural surroundings.

How the space is defined, use of lighting, levels and materials

Whatever space is used and whatever its configuration, it will be defined either by a physical barrier, such as the front row of seats or a wall, or light will be used to define the area that will be used by the actors. More and more stage spaces are on more than one level, with the play making use of different levels for different scenes. Other materials include the use of back-projection and video images to create atmosphere or add to the plot. Sometimes the whole space is identified only by light.

How do you describe where you are on the stage?

The standard method is to describe positions from the point of view of the performer, standing on the stage and looking at the audience. The plan below shows the expressions used.

UP RIGHT	UP CENTRE	UP LEFT
CENTRE RIGHT	CENTRE STAGE	CENTRE LEFT
DOWN RIGHT	DOWN CENTRE	DOWN LEFT

AUDIENCE

Designing sets for drama spaces

Once the director has decided what style will be used in the drama, and upon the space where it will be presented, there will be a discussion with the designer to pass on the director's ideas. The designer will have some artistic input into this, suggesting the best way the director's ideas might be put into practice. To do this, the designer needs a form of communication to pass on ideas. This is done through two simple types of sketch.

The first is called the **designer's sketch**. For this, imagine you are looking at the space for the drama from the point of view of the audience. What do you see? This is what the designer's sketch will show, a picture of the acting space and what will be on it.

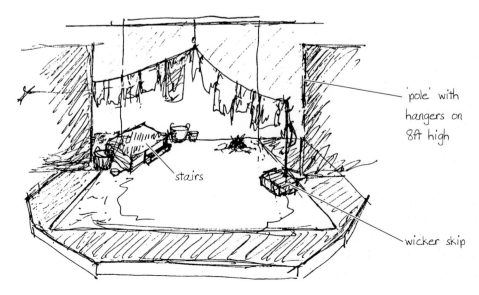

Setting for studio production of *Don Quixote* – Leicestershire Schools production

'pole' with hangers on 8ft high

stairs

wicker skip

The second is called the **ground plan**. Imagine you are up in the air, looking down on the drama space. Imagine the set and furniture is in place. What you see is the view the designer draws from the point in the air looking down.

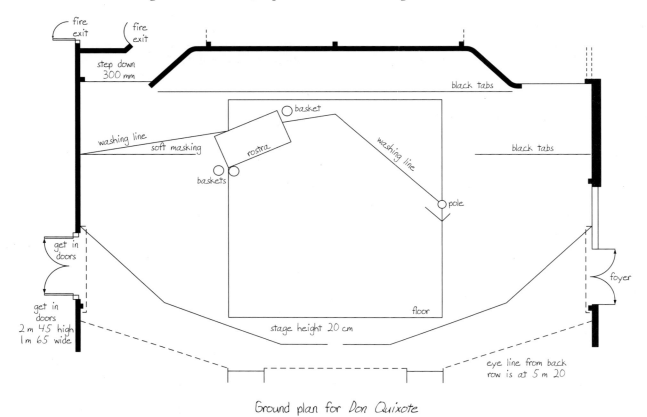

Ground plan for *Don Quixote*

What are the examiners looking for?

➤ three different types of staging
➤ how they can be used
➤ what the potential is for each type

➤ what the restrictions are, and how flexible they are
➤ the implications for designers and performers.

Tasks and challenges

- Imagine you are the director who has been asked to present the play for which scenario A on page 51 is the summary, at a theatre that has in-the-round staging. Describe your ideas for this. If possible, work with a group and improvise a scene based on the scenario, doing it in the round.
- Choose any script that you have been working on. Have a go at some ideas for a set. Draw a designer's sketch and a ground plan. Do not worry if you cannot draw very well. Use labels to make sure everything can be understood.

Although the specification only requires you to know about three spaces or venues, it is recommended that these three be contrasting ones. Know how each one poses different challenges for the deviser, designer, director and performer.

Want to know more? Research and extras

- Find out about the origins of the word 'proscenium' by investigating Greek theatre. What did a Greek theatre look like?
- Discover what you can about some British theatres with a particular type of staging:
  - the original Traverse Theatre in Edinburgh
  - the New Victoria Theatre in Stoke-on-Trent (in the round) and its former building, the Victoria in Hanley
  - the Stephen Joseph Theatre in Scarborough (home to Alan Ayckbourn, playwright).
- What were the main features of the Restoration stage?
- How were medieval mystery plays staged? Which of the types of staging listed in this section most closely fit the way they were presented?
- Why do we use the expressions 'up' and 'down' when describing the position of a performer or piece of furniture on the stage acting space?
- Take a play or a devised piece you have been working on and suggest how the space might be defined by light, sound, furniture and props only. Do not use scenery, or a normal stage layout.

Area of study 5 – Improvisation

What does the specification say?

Area of study 5	Improvisation
Minimum requirements	*Must experience both spontaneous and polished improvisation*
Definition	Unscripted performance which relies on the performer's ability to extemporise; to create spontaneously.
Examples	Used as part of the devising process, or as part of workshop activity. A feature of medieval mystery plays; *lazzi* in *commedia dell'arte*; some fringe theatre. Using a variety of exercises to develop confidence in improvisation. Giving work dramatic integrity so it matches intention.

What does it mean?

Improvisation is a word used a great deal by those involved in creating drama. At its simplest level, improvisation is performance that is not scripted and that relies on the ability of the performers to make it up as they go along.

When this is happening without any preparation at all, and is an instant response to an idea, character, situation or stimulus, it is described as **spontaneous improvisation**.

1 Look at the picture on page 32. In small groups, respond to it with some action, without discussion or planning. Each person should take on the role of any of the people in the photograph. See how long you can keep the scene going before it either breaks down or gets silly!

When improvisation happens as part of the process of exploring an idea, and is gone over several times, on each occasion perhaps including elements of the previous improvisation, but always trying to improve the outcome, it is known as **polished improvisation**.

2 Look at the picture above. What do you think the actor in this picture is trying to express? In a group, discuss what ideas might be used to develop a scene. Try one or more of these ideas out. Repeat the best one, **editing**, **adapting** and **adding** to improve the quality. Repeat it until you are happy you have a piece of drama that communicates your idea successfully. You could also repeat this process for the picture opposite.

Improvisation may be used to get ideas in response to a stimulus, to explore a text, to develop a role, for rehearsal or as a performance in its own right.

3 In the polished improvisation you were trying out earlier, you took on a role. Let the other members of the group question you about your role. Stay in character and try to answer the questions truthfully as the character you have chosen to be. Sometimes you will have to think about what your character may do, or has done; you will have to invent a history for her or him, and know little details like age and likes and dislikes.

This exercise is sometimes called **hot-seating**, and is a useful technique to use when preparing a drama or exploring a text.

What are the examiners looking for?

The examiners will want to know that you know what the word 'improvisation' means and that you understand the terms 'spontaneous' and 'polished'. They will want you to know when to use improvisation. The examiners will also expect you to have taken part in lots of improvisation, as both Unit 1 and Unit 2 require drama activity that relies on its use.

Tasks and challenges

- Repeat the hot-seating exercise but with a character from a play you have studied. Create two different ways of taking on the role in a performance of the play. You will find that the character begins to grow and to develop some depth. Try this with the roles reversed, e.g. with the man at home and the woman going to work.

- Try out this improvisation, which works best with a mixed group of at least seven. One of your group will need to act as director.

    Set out a few simple pieces of furniture and decide as a group where things will be. The context is the kitchen and front door and hallway of a house. Inside the house when the action starts is a woman. She has just seen the children off to school, and is making a drink. There is a knock at the door and the next-door neighbour walks in without waiting to be invited, and sits herself down for a drink.

    From this point on the director tells the other members of the group when to enter the scene, and what is wanted from them. The director could introduce some unusual happenings, such as the milkman/woman knocking and demanding payment for milk for a lengthy period; the arrival of an old boyfriend; the appearance of the husband's secretary to collect some clothes for a sudden business trip; and so on. The director should secretly tell the new character who they are, what they are to do, how long to stay, and whether they are to get rid of any of the characters still 'on stage'. The director can introduce anything she or he wants, such as a large package arriving suddenly. Once a character is established, that character may enter or exit when necessary.

- Have another look at one of the improvisations you did earlier. As a group, make sure you are all familiar with what you did. Now apply to it the things talked about in areas of study 1, 2, 3 and 4. Look at what it is the examiner will want you to know, and see if you can apply it to the improvisation. Note down the decisions you make.

- Take one of your improvisations and see how you might enhance it by using one or more design elements such as light, make-up or costume.

> ## TOP TIPS
>
> Do not be casual in the use of the word 'improvisation'. When including anything in your portfolio about it, be precise as to how and why you are using it.
>
> Show that you know how improvisation can be used to explore text and help understanding of what is going on in a play.
>
> Use it to develop characters, both in understanding them and in creating a role for performance.

Want to know more? Research and extras

The specification gives some examples of drama where improvisation has been used. Find out what you can about them.

- The first is 'a feature of medieval mystery plays'. These plays were performed in the street and usually moved from stage to stage, a bit like promenade theatre. See what you can discover about the way improvisation might have been used.

- The second is '*lazzi* in *commedia dell'arte*'. *Lazzi* is the plural of *lazzo*. The word *lazzo* is used to describe the improvisation that took place around the text by the players in *commedia dell'arte*. It might include bits of stage business, verbal cleverness or word play, tricks or showing-off of skills, and adding bits of made-up text, usually called 'ad libs'. Information about the content of *commedia dell'arte* is harder to find, but see what you can discover.

- The third is 'some fringe theatre'. Improvisation became very popular as a form at fringe theatre events such as the Edinburgh Festival Fringe. There are some television shows that rely on live improvisation where the presenters respond to questions from the audience. Can you find any companies that use improvisation extensively as a core part of their performances?

- If you want to explore the theory of improvisation, Viola Spolin wrote a book called *Improvisation* that you might find interesting.

Area of study 6 – Genre, style and convention

What does the specification say?

Area of study 6	Genre, style and convention
Minimum requirements	*Candidates must study and understand more than one genre, more than one style, and be conversant enough with the conventions listed in the examples to select and employ them in their devised work, and relate them to their understanding of script*
Definition	A kind or style of arts activity, usually characterised by the nature of its subject matter or its style of presentation or performance. May be linked to a historical period, or to a particular company or group of practitioners. Implicit agreement of understanding between deviser, performer and audience on the set of conventions and codes to be used.
Examples	**Genre**: comedy; tragedy; kitchen sink; melodrama; documentary; theatre-in-education; agitprop; historical period such as Greek or Restoration; *commedia dell'arte*. **Style:** naturalistic; non-naturalistic; abstract; representational; didactic; masked. Sometimes a genre will be used to describe a style, e.g. an actor delivering a speech in a melodramatic way. **Conventions:** ritual ceremony; mimed activities; still image; narration; interviews; meetings; re-enactments; sound tracking; thought tracking; reportage; giving witness; collective drawing; telephone conversations; overheard conversations; simulations; mantle of the expert; diaries; letters; defining space; costuming games; role on the wall; analogy; journals; messages; folk forms; noises off; making maps; caption making; role reversal; hot-seating; prepared roles; interrogations; marking the moment. **Theatrical conventions:** ghost(s); stock characters; dramatic irony; allegorical narrative; prologue; epilogue.

What does it mean?

Sometimes, the meanings of words in drama lead to discussion, debate and even disagreement. Genre and style are words that have stimulated such debate. For the purpose of this specification and your examination, the words have been defined, and it is the meanings given here that will be used by examiners when awarding marks.

Genre

Genre describes what type of drama is being enacted. It usually relates to the content. The specification provides some examples.

Comedy

Lots of drama would probably come under this heading. The Greeks defined one group of their plays using this heading, and the word has been used to describe content that is 'uplifting' and 'optimistic'. It is more usual today for the word to be qualified with another word describing the sort of comedy. So we have:

Comedy of manners – gets its humour from observation of the way characters behave; it is usually set in a historical period when there may have been strict rules of social behaviour.

1 Comedy of manners could be applied to any period in history. Try and devise a short drama that draws its comedy from the observation of a group of modern-day people.

Black comedy – gets its humour from the macabre and gruesome.

2 Think of something gruesome and devise a short scene based on it that has a comic outcome or comic treatment. Be aware of the boundaries of good taste, and the sensitivity of people when dealing with gruesome or macabre things. This is a useful application of area of study 3, audience.

Low comedy – there is a reliance on the vulgar and the coarse; the comedy is unlikely to come about through clever wit or detailed characterisation, but through obvious means like clowning and jokes.

3 Devise a short scene in this genre. Be careful that it does not turn into **slapstick**, which is a different type of comedy. Make sure that you keep control, and that what you devise is funny for an audience rather than just funny for those taking part. As with black comedy, there is a need to keep in mind what is acceptable to an audience, especially in the context of a public examination where work should be suitable for general audiences.

High comedy – sophisticated, usually set in high social class situations, where the comedy comes from detail of characterisation, the cleverness of the language and use of wit.

Romantic comedy – although usually applied to plays where the subject is love and it all ends happily, it can also be used of plays where sentiment is at the core, and even to plays that have highly imaginative content.

This is a drama that has a serious subject, with a sad, unhappy or disastrous ending. It often takes for its subject an event or series of events that have unhappy consequences. The Greeks used tragedy as their major form of drama, although their meaning for the word was not quite the same. In the Greek sense there would often be a battle with fate, and fate would win: man could not escape what the Gods had decided. There would be a serious exploration of an event, usually of historical or contemporary significance.

4 Think of a modern-day event or series of events that could provide the subject for a tragedy. Prepare a brief scenario.

Note: Shakespeare's plays are often divided into tragedies and comedies.

Kitchen sink

Arnold Wesker and Harold Pinter are among those playwrights who have had their work described by this term. It refers to a type of drama that developed as a reaction to the **context** that provided most of the settings for plays in the 1940s and 1950s – middle-class, drawing-room, polite drama. Kitchen sink drama could be set anywhere, including the kitchen, uses realistic language, involves the working class, and uses anything at all for its content.

Kitchen sink drama: a scene from John Osborne's *Look Back in Anger* (at the Littleton/National Theatre, 1999)

5 Look at scenario G on page 54. Revise it, setting it in an ordinary home. Improvise two dramas: the first using the scenario as written; the second using your revised version.

Consider how you will approach the characters and how the way they speak and behave will be influenced by the context. If you were to perform one of these dramas, how would you stage it? How would you define the performance space?

Melodrama

Although it was music that gave melodrama its original name – words accompanied by music – it is its content and style that has given it a distinctive quality as a genre in Britain. At its height during the 1800s, it had a number of recognisable features:

- content that was often based on a true story
- romance
- violence
- good battling against evil
- often the working class being taken advantage of by the upper class
- sensational happenings
- justice coming out on top
- wrongdoers getting their just desserts
- stock characters such as the evil gentleman as the villain, the old parents, country yokels, the maiden wronged by the villain, the policeman
- emotional moments.

Religion, morals and the law were upheld in these plays, and in the happy ending it had to be clear that wrong did not win, and that the villain was dealt with. Usually, the villain would confess his guilt and express remorse.

Today, melodrama is often considered as comedy where the actors over-act and shout and declaim, and no one really takes it seriously. This is very different from when it was first performed, with serious matters as content. People would react and respond to the violent portrayal of death and would identify with characters who were being done down. Playwrights would often try to shock their audience. The content of Victorian melodrama was a good reflection of social class.

In many ways, it could be said that melodrama had a similar function to modern-day tabloid newspapers.

> **6** What sort of people would provide stock characters today? Try and think of three examples across social classes and from different backgrounds. Devise a short scene where some of your stock characters meet together unexpectedly.

Documentary theatre

This genre is looked at in area of study 3, audience (see page 21). It is very much of the second half of the twentieth century, and Joan Littlewood's *Oh What a Lovely War* is one of the best examples. It is theatre that attempts to look at an event or issue through the provision of evidence, filling in the lack of knowledge with educated guesses. Sometimes the focus of documentary theatre may be something that is about to happen in a community, and the drama is an attempt to demonstrate it would be a mistake, drawing on research and resources to show a picture based on evidence.

Theatre-in-education

This genre is discussed in area of study 3, audience (see page 21). It is popular, and has very definite aims. The style of presentation needs to fit the nature of the audience very carefully.

Agitprop

Agitprop is tied up with political theatre, and is considered in area of study 3, audience (see page 22). It is theatre where the main function is to make a political point, to address a perceived social wrong, or to create a change in society through influencing large numbers of people. The name 'agitprop' comes from the words 'agitation' and 'propaganda'. There is some further work on agitprop in section B (see page 77).

History

History plays tell a tale of or from a historical period. Some of Shakespeare's plays are sometimes referred to as the Histories.

Restoration

King Charles II was restored to the throne in 1660, and it is this event that gives this genre its name. Plays in this era have very specific features, usually related to the comedy of manners.

Commedia dell'arte

Developed in Italy in the sixteenth century, this genre spread across Europe. Mainly improvised drama, it has stock characters and uses masks, tumbling and other skills of a physical nature. Some modern playwrights, including Berkoff, claim to be influenced by its form.

Style

This specification uses the word 'style' to describe how a drama might be performed. The following examples are given.

Naturalistic

Naturalism and realism are two words not always easily distinguished. As far as this specification is concerned, the term 'naturalism' or 'naturalistic' means that the drama is devised and presented on the basis that the action is to be believed in as as if it was something that was really happening.

So movements, words, set and scenery, furniture and props, costume and make-up are done in such a way as to support this. It treats the audience as if

Example of a naturalistic set, from John Bowen's *Siege of Oak Tree Tea Rooms*

they were peeping in through the keyhole, or as if the division between stage and audience was a wall impervious to the actors, but see-through for the audience.

The audience 'suspend their disbelief' and come to identify with and believe in the characters and the setting presented to them.

> **7** Look at scenario A on page 51. What approach might the director and designer have in preparing for a performance?

Non-naturalistic

In this style, the drama is presented in a way that does not require the audience to believe in the characters or in what is happening. The audience is there as observers or commentators, witnessing and experiencing rather than becoming part of what is going on. Playwrights and directors use a variety of techniques to achieve this. These may include:

- using back-projection
- having set and props that are exaggerated
- taking a minimalist approach to setting without any attempt to reproduce a real-life setting
- the actor addressing the audience directly
- the actor using exaggerated movements or gestures
- dialogue not reproducing natural patterns of speech.

There is often a reason for not wanting the audience to empathise and using non-naturalistic techniques. For example, in political theatre it will be the message that the playwright wants to put across.

> **8** Look at Scenario E on page 53. Imagine that this piece of drama was going to be produced as a piece to make fun of people who gamble, and to point out the misery it can cause. What ideas might you have for presentation that would prevent the drama from being naturalistic?

Abstract

This style uses contexts that may be unusual, and will have non-naturalistic settings. Structure will not be standard, and there may be no pattern to it. There may not be a plot, and characterisation will be uneven, with the characters serving the idea being presented rather than any idea of story. The intention may be to present a series of ideas, or to provide an experience for the audience to go through. There may be a series of images about which the audience will come to its own conclusion. A genre that uses this sort of style is theatre of the absurd. Samuel Beckett and Eugene Ionesco are two playwrights who use this sort of approach in some of their plays.

Representational

This style uses characters, and perhaps setting and props, as symbols, representing an idea. This is quite a useful style to use during improvisation. At its extreme it could be said to become allegory. The medieval play *Everyman* is an example of allegory (see scenario C on page 52).

Masked

Masks have been a part of drama for a long time. In early Greek drama they were very important, as they were in *commedia dell'arte*. In more recent times, Brecht and other contemporary playwrights made use of them. Modern-day use is quite extensive with certain companies. One company, Trading Faces, bases its annual repertoire on physical theatre, with mask work an essential part.

Masked characters in *The Man Who Woke Up in the Dark* by Trading Faces

Physical theatre

This style of drama came about as a response to a heavy emphasis on text and words in drama during the twentieth century. It focuses on movement and visual images, using the person of the actor flexibly, perhaps to represent meaning or as a symbol. Some companies that specialise in this sort of style have actors who are very fit, as they are required to undertake very athletic moves. Some moves the actors make are similar to those of clowns, tumblers and gymnasts. There has also been a narrowing of the gap between contemporary dance and drama through the medium of physical theatre.

9 In Steven Berkoff's play *Metamorphosis* (based on the novel by Kafka), one of the characters, Gregor, turns into a beetle. He does this on stage, and does not use a disguising costume. The actor represents the beetle through his moves, positions and stances. Devise a short scene where each one of your group slowly turns into an animal or insect. Focus on the physical nature of what you do, the moves, speech, gestures and expressions.

Conventions

The term 'conventions' is used in two ways in this specification.

First it is used to describe things that are agreed by deviser, designer, director, performer and audience, often about the way something will happen. For example, in a piece of modern-day drama, there may be several characters in the acting space. A moment arrives when only one character is required to deliver a short monologue. The other characters could leave, but are required to return very soon. Rather than disrupt the drama with unnecessary movement, it may be that the director will instruct the other characters to stand aside and turn their back on the audience, remaining perfectly still. The other characters know and understand what this means, and so does the audience. All concerned accept what is happening. This is a convention.

Another example is when characters help change the set. They may not be acting in role, but the audience accept the convention that they are preparing for the next scene and ignore them.

Second, there is the set of conventions used for devising and exploring in drama activity where there may be no audience. Conventions may be used to help develop character or role, understand script, explore a sub-text or generate additional ideas. Some conventions used in this way are listed in the specification and are repeated below. These are examples only, as there are many such conventions used by those working in drama.

- ritual ceremony
- narration
- re-enactments
- reportage
- telephone conversations
- mantle of the expert
- defining space
- analogy
- folk forms
- caption making
- prepared roles
- mimed activities
- interviews
- sound-tracking
- giving witness
- overheard conversations
- diaries
- costuming games
- journals
- noises off
- role reversal
- interrogations
- still image
- meetings
- thought-tracking
- collective drawing
- simulations
- letters
- role on the wall
- messages
- making maps
- hot-seating
- marking the moment

10 Using conventions such as those listed on page 43 can be a very valuable way of improving your drama. Keep a record of those you use, explaining what you did and how you used it. You may want to use a table like the one below for this purpose. It could be included as part of your portfolio evidence.

Convention	Explanation	How I used it

What are the examiners looking for?

Examiners want to know that you know how to apply a range of genre, styles and conventions. It is not enough just to know some names. You need to know what each one means, how it is used, or what its features are.

You must know more than one of each genre and style well. Get into the habit when devising work of talking about what genre and/or style you are going to use, so that it becomes part of your natural process of devising.

When looking at scripts, or watching live performances, identify the genre and style and try to recognise how it has determined the nature of performance.

As for conventions, become familiar with the list and use many of them in your work. When preparing work for the practical examination and for the written paper, remember to use conventions in the exploration and development process, and to refer to them in writing your answers or in your portfolio.

Tasks and challenges

- Look through some tabloid newspapers and see if you can find a story that reminds you of the story in scenario H on page 55. Prepare your own scenario for a modern-day melodrama and improvise a scene from it. Think about the stock characters you could use that would be relevant to an audience today. How would you shock the audience, and how would you get them emotionally involved?

- Present a series of images on a theme you have chosen that will provide an experience for an audience, and does not have a plot or defined characters. If you want, combine some features of physical theatre with your final piece.

TOP TIPS

It is useful for you to be able to record your experience of the same genre or style in drama work you have:

- studied as a script
- seen performed
- worked on yourself as devised pieces.

This will demonstrate that you have had experience of the same genre or style in different contexts.

Use the table to keep a log of conventions used and their effectiveness. Become expert in two or three so that you can use those as examples of successful ways of developing drama. Almost everyone knows about hot-seating, so use others as well and do not rely on one convention.

When writing about genre, refer to features of the genre rather than just using the name.

Want to know more? Research and extras

- Censorship is something that has affected plays and theatres throughout the ages. Investigate censorship and the patents of theatres during the early 1800s.
- It has been suggested that the Greek Satyr plays are similar to what we now might call 'low comedy'. What you can find out about the content and method of performance of the Satyr play?
- Use the Internet to find out the story behind Maria Marten and the Murder in the Red Barn.
- Look into the use of masks in Greek theatre.
- What is the form of drama called a masque?

Area of study 7 – The semiotics of drama and theatre

What does the specification say?

Area of study 7	The semiotics of drama and theatre
Minimum requirements	*An understanding of the actor as sign; proxemics; symbols in set and properties*
Definition	How meaning is created and communicated through systems of encodable and decodable signs and symbols.
Examples	The actor as sign. The way dialogue is structured to signal content. Verse and prose. The function of a character. Proxemics. Constructing stage 'pictures' – setting, costume, properties, lighting – in relation to the facial and physical work of the actor. Stage directions and their relationship with set and bringing an intended image alive. Links with structure and shaping, and with character, context and plot.

What does it mean?

Semiotics? Sounds a bit of a scary word! Once you get to grips with it, however, you will see that it helps to draw lots of things in drama together. It is a word used at A level, so having some early understanding of it will be helpful for the future too.

The specification explains semiotics as 'How meaning is created and communicated through systems of encodable and decodable signs and symbols.' Put more simply, semiotics is the signs and symbols of drama.

The specification goes on to provide some examples. These are quite specific and give us a good framework for study. They can be grouped into four sections; the actor as sign; proxemics; constructing stage pictures; stage directions.

The actor as sign

The functions of a character will be various. In extract A on page 56, for example, the character John has several functions. He is the father figure, and perhaps represents a particular kind of parent. He also represents a husband or partner and, depending on how he presents the role, there will be messages about that role. Is it stereotypical, does it represent the current views of society? And what about him being out of work? Is he representing the impact on people who are unemployed? If he is all of these things, an audience cannot look at him just as 'John', but as a character representing these different functions. Sometimes the name of the character will have a meaning, and this may be played upon or made use of within the text.

The way dialogue is structured may signal content and different sorts of meaning. So may the use of verse and prose. Why is it that Shakespeare switches from verse to prose during a play? Why does Godber use verse?

1 Traditionally, verse has been associated with tragedy and prose with comedy. Choose a piece of verse from any Shakespeare play and have a try at turning it into prose. Does it still communicate effectively? If you know of another play, perhaps a modern one, that uses verse you might try the same exercise.

The usual form of dialogue is that characters take turns to speak, and within their speeches they identify issues of importance, provide information about people not there, about events in the past or events yet to come. The way the dialogue is structured can tell us something about the character. Does one person take control of the scene, become dominant? Does this signify anything about their character or what might happen in the future?

2 Look at extract A on page 56. Is there anything in the words used that suggests who might be the power figure, if there is one?

When the language used between characters does not move the action forward, or does not add to the knowledge of the audience concerning the context or the character, perhaps the playwright is trying to make a point.

3 Look at extract B on page 57. What is going on? What messages are there for an audience?

Rule-breaking devices are used by playwrights to make a point.

Caryl Churchill uses overlapping dialogue to:

- point up the use of the word 'I' and identify a collective female image
- speed up the pace of the drama
- develop tension.

She also writes dialogue in such a way that apparently sophisticated people come out with outrageous expressions that may seem the opposite of their character, to give a pointer, to indicate a message or to give a sign.

Proxemics

This word is used to describe the meaning of the relationship in space between a character and another character, a character and an object or a character and a piece of set.

4 Work with one other person. Face them and say 'What do you think?' Now have your partner sit on a chair while you pace up and down behind them and repeat the line. Then place them sitting on the floor and lean over them threateningly. Finally, say it to their face, your face only inches away from theirs. Notice how the way you position yourselves affects the way you say the line. Develop two short improvisations using the line, one with the two of you in a very relaxed position, and the other with one of you in a very threatening position.

You can change the whole meaning of a scene and give a different message about the relationship between characters, just through the positioning of characters in this way.

Constructing stage 'pictures'

Use of setting, costume, properties and lighting in relation to the facial and physical work of the actor.

If we read comics we experience a form of communication that relies on a still picture. Action might be suggested by the positioning of characters in the picture, but in itself, the picture is still. Cartoons in newspapers and magazines have the same impact. Through a still image they tell us something. Sometimes there may be a caption or a word bubble, but the best cartoons are those where there are no words. The picture tells the story.

One of the most powerful still images that can influence our lives is the advertisement. Often, without words, a smile will be brought to our faces, or we may be shocked by the message.

If we apply this to drama, we have another example of semiotics in action. The message may be put across through a stage picture, possibly using proxemics, and using many other aspects of drama. Characters will be positioned, gestures may be used, particular expressions on faces decided upon. If the deviser or director wants to put across a particular point, all of these will be thought about. This is semiotics in action.

5 In groups, imagine you have been performing a piece of drama on the horrors of war. You want to end the drama with a still image that summarises the effect of the horrors of war on all sorts of people: soldiers, their families, ordinary people in towns, cities and villages. Devise this still image. Think about props and what sort of background you would want. Then decide what style it is going to be in. Will it be naturalistic or not? What use might you make of light and/or sound? Try to identify each element of your stage picture and what message, what meaning it will have.

Stage directions

Stage directions and their relationship with set can be used in many ways to help with meaning and bringing an intended image alive. In a script, stage directions may help the way a character develops a role and performs it. Examples include:

- identifying the character with a description
- giving details of occupation, age and practical matters
- providing clues as to attitudes of one character to another
- giving movement
- defining action to be taken
- defining reaction to another character's words or actions
- describing facial expression
- indicating quality of voice, the tone in which something is said
- using emotion

- the pace at which a line is delivered
- the volume to be used in delivering a line
- the rhythm to be used in delivering the line
- any emphasis to be used
- any mannerisms the character has
- asides
- pauses.

A similar approach can be used with design:

- the setting – where it is
- levels and areas
- the whole stage picture
- time of day and season
- the weather
- costume – distinctive requirements
- mood (lighting and sound).

6 Look at a text that has stage directions. Find examples for as many of the items in the two lists above as you can.

What are the examiners looking for?

What is important here is not the words but the meaning. Examiners will be looking to see if you have grasped the concept of meanings being passed on to an audience through decisions you make, as:

deviser – looking at meaning being passed on through the words to be used, characters involved, or symbols

designer – interpreting the meaning in ways that will communicate to an audience through aspects of design

director – taking on the responsibility for making sure the sign system works, that everyone has thought about what is communicated and how methods of presentation can affect the audience's understanding

performer – using the tools of an actor to communicate effectively to an audience in a way that reflects the director's and playwright's intentions.

They will want to know that you understand how meaning can be seen in how the actor acts and speaks, and in their positioning. They will want to be assured that you understand the concept of the 'whole stage picture' and the meaning that can be transmitted from it.

Tasks and challenges

- Look at extract C on page 57. In each of the seven versions a different word is highlighted. Work on a short improvisation of a scene involving two or three characters in which the extract is spoken. Try it out with the different emphasis on the word highlighted. Notice how it changes the meaning of the scene. This is semiotics at work in script. The meaning changes depending upon how the words are said.

- Devise a scene from any stimulus. Make the words you say naturalistic. Then develop actions to emphasise what you are saying. Make moves and gestures. Exaggerate them to underline the meaning of the words you are saying. How does it feel to act like this? What would be the impact upon an audience?

TOP TIPS

Become familiar with, and use, the words **semiotics** and **proxemics**.

Spot semiotics at work in plays you have studied, not only in the creation and direction of your own devised work. When recording evidence, make reference to signs and symbols that were effective in drama you have seen or read.

Make it clear in your portfolio and in written paper and practical examination that you have thought about signs and symbols in your work, and what might be transmitted to the audience. Link this with the intention of the deviser, whether playwright or candidate.

When you are writing your own scripts, or extracts, make sure you use stage directions in the way described above, to help transmit meaning.

Want to know more? Research and extras

- A number of people have written about sign systems in the theatre. See if you can find out about the Pavis Questionnaire (see bibliography: Pavis, P. *Theatre Analysis*). It was designed for drama students with little or no knowledge of semiotics.
- Are there any examples of semiotics in the way theatres are built or organised? Think about the theatre buildings of the Greeks, the Victorians, and the modern day.
- Consider the sentence 'What on earth do you think you are doing?' How many ways can you find to present this line so that it has a different meaning? Can you find four, or more? Consider use of voice, proxemics, location and lighting. Note down your ideas in a copy of the grid below.

Idea	Use of voice	Proxemics	Location	Lighting
1				
2				
3				
4				

- Look at extract D on page 58. Use all you have learned about semiotics to make this short extract effective in performance.

The Scenarios and Extracts that follow have been gathered together as resources that students working through Section A can refer to. For ease of reference the resources have been cross-referenced to the pages that mention them. However, the intention is that teachers and students can refer to and use these resources at any point during the course of their work.

Scenarios

The Burglar (see pages 11, 13, 41)

It was dark. The night was disturbed only by the dripping of the rain from broken gutters. The man crept quietly along the wall that divided the garden from the footpath. He stopped, listened, then moved on. He limped slightly, and as the light from a passing car shone on his face, the eyes looked frightened, the expression careworn.
5 Quickly he climbed over the wall where there was a gap where some bricks had crumbled away. Squelching on the wet grass, he approached the rear of the house. All was in darkness. Yes, the window was open again. He had noticed the other day when passing that it had been left open. Probably the hot days recently had made the owners careless. He climbed in, careful not to knock the plant off the ledge. With his torch he
10 crossed the kitchen into the hall, and turned into a room on his left. It was a study. Perhaps there would be some money on the desk. He sat on the chair, put the torch at his side, and started rummaging, looking for money, or anything he could use.

A noise startled him, and before he could identify it, the light was turned on. 'And what do you think you are doing?' asked the stern but not unkind voice. The face that looked
15 up was full of desperation and hopelessness.

B The Head (see pages 9, 13)

I was busting! Not just wanting to go, but absolutely busting! I didn't think 'the Doc' would let me out of class, but something in my face must have told him that I wasn't trying it on, that I really needed to go.

I hurried along the corridor. There was always something a bit exciting about walking
5 along corridors when everyone else was in lessons. It sort of gave you a buzz.

Just as I came to the corner, I heard noises, then glass tinkling, then the sound of a bell. It wasn't lesson change yet, there was at least half an hour to go. What was going on? I soon found out as I turned the corner, saw glass on the floor, by the wall, just underneath the fire alarm button, and heard running footsteps round the next corner.
10 I stood petrified, looking at the damage, hearing the bell destroying the calm. I was transfixed. Then came the voice.

'Robinson!' it thundered. 'Robinson, come here!'

It was the Head.

C Everyman (see pages 13, 17, 42)

This was a play written in medieval times as a warning to people about the way they behaved. Almost everybody believed in God, and was frightened of what might happen to them if they did not do what God wanted. Like most people, however, their good intentions often disappeared and this play was a reminder about how they should
5 behave, and a warning of what might happen if they did not change their ways. It was called a morality play, and is an allegory. What follows is a brief summary of the play.

The play starts with God telling his messenger that he is fed up with humankind, because they have forgotten him and are behaving badly. He sends the messenger for Death to have an accounting of Everyman. The character Everyman is, as the name
10 suggests, meant to represent the whole of humanity.

Death is then sent off to find Everyman and to bring him for a 'reckoning'. When Everyman receives the visit from Death, he is dismayed, and asks for a delay, which is not granted. He asks if he can take someone with him to the reckoning, the final judgement, and Death says that he can. Everyman decides to go to his friends, his family
15 and his wealth. He asks each in turn about the good time they have had together. He asks each of them if they will do anything for him, and each of them say they will. Once Everyman reveals that they will have to die to go with him, they all desert him.

Finally, Everyman goes to his Good Deeds to see if she will go with him. Unfortunately Good Deeds is so weak she can barely stand, because Everyman has done so little that
20 is good, and it seems impossible for her to help him. Everyman says he is sorry and pays penance for what he has done, whipping himself. As he does this, Good Deeds gets stronger and accompanies Everyman to the final judgement.

D The place of women (see page 11)

It was a lovely sunny morning. It was a Saturday. The man was reading the paper, sitting at the breakfast table. His wife was sitting opposite, trying to read the front page of her husband's paper. There was a pleasant, happy atmosphere.

The woman pours herself another coffee, asks her husband if he wants one. He grunts
5 assent, and she pours. He asks her, from behind the paper, how the children got on at school during the week. She replies that they had done very well and were enjoying their time at school. She obviously has something else she wants to say, and hurriedly goes on to talk about how much more confident they are, and how nice it is to have them at school and not to have to think about picking them up and dropping them off
10 now they are so much older.

Plucking up courage, she then suggests that as the children do not need her now during the school day, she thought she might get a little part-time job. She says she has seen an advert in the paper for a job that she thought she would enjoy. The paper is slowly lowered ...

E *All's well that ends well* (see pages 15, 18, 41)

The young man was delighted. To be trusted for the first time with the money to go and buy the lottery ticket for the syndicate at work! It might not seem much, but it was a lot of money, and it was usually the section leader who did that. And it was working time, too, not his own time. If he took it steady, it would take half an hour to get there and back,
5 better than all that paperwork stacked up on his desk.

They all waved him off, as if recognising it was an adventure for him. Who knows, perhaps this would be the time that they won, and it would be him who had paid for the tickets!

He checked to make sure he had the card with the set of numbers in his pocket: yes, it was there. Same numbers every week, paid on Tuesday for both the Wednesday and the
10 Saturday draw. Fifty-eight pounds, one pound for each person in the section. The money was hot in his hand, the curled up notes seeming almost to have a life of their own.

The newsagents was suddenly there before him, all too quickly. In he went, paid in the money and gave over the card. The girl serving him made some comment about training a new retriever for the money run. She must have been the one usually here on a Tuesday
15 and was used to someone else paying in. He didn't care. The task was done. He took the ticket with the numbers on and began to move away. His eye caught the advert for an 'Instant'. His hand went into his pocket, out came a two-pound coin, and before he knew what he was doing, he was handing it over for one of the cards that promised a fortune. 'And I'll have a chocolate bar please.' His eyes were fixed on the Instant as he left the shop,
20 almost colliding with someone who hesitated, as if she knew him, but he didn't look up, too engrossed in the wording on the back of the card. He decided to save it until he was home, opening the chocolate wrapper, clumsily dropping it and his card, and stuffing the chocolate wrapper into his pocket as he hurried back to work.

As he approached the street where his office was located, he realised he wasn't holding
25 the lottery ticket. Must be in his pocket, he thought. A search revealed the chocolate wrapper, but no lottery ticket. His steps slowed as he got closer to the office. Where was it? Where had it gone? He looked around, but the street was clear except for a girl who seemed vaguely familiar walking back the same way he had come.

It did not matter how much he searched. He had just to accept it. He had lost it. His steps
30 were now down to a positive crawl, and he was inside the building, only seconds away from the office. Just have to face the music.

In he went, heads turned to see who it was, faces looking at him expectantly. 'Pay it in OK?' asked the team leader.

'Yes,' he replied.

35 'Why do you look as if you've just seen a ghost then?' asked the woman who worked at the same desk as him.

'Because, because,' have to tell them, no way out, 'I've lost the ticket!'

Silence. Everyone still, eyes fixed on him. The ultimate crime.

Just as the tension reached a pitch where he felt he would have to scream or run, a voice
40 behind him from the door said, 'And still lost it would be if I hadn't seen you in the shop. Near knocked me over you did, so taken up with your Instant and your chocolate bar. Dropped it in the doorway you did, so I picked it up.'

'Sally ... Sally ... oh thank you, Sally, and I'm sorry I knocked you over and didn't see you and ... oh thank you!' The relief was so obviously enormous that several of the older
45 workers had kind smiles on their faces. Sally picked up the Instant, which he had dropped on the floor in his agitation, and started fiddling with it.

'Well, you just be grateful, and take more care in future.' Bill was about to lecture him when Sally, herself as white as a sheet, staggered to a desk and slumped in the chair.

'Why, what is it lass?' began Bill.

50 'It's ...Well he may have lost the lottery ticket, but he's only gone and won on the Instant.'

'How much?' asked Bill incredulously.

'You'll never believe it.' She fixed the young man with a stare:

'You've won ...'

(This extract can be used with the characters playing male or female roles.)

F *Waiting for Godot* by Samuel Beckett, written in 1948, first performed in 1953 (see page 19)

Two men, Vladimir and Estragon, live in hope of the arrival of a mysterious being, called Godot. Although Godot sends messages that he is delayed, he never comes. The whole play consists of their waiting, passing time, just existing, meeting only two other characters, Pozzo and Lucky.

G *Breakfast with Mary* (see page 38)

It is a lovely sunny day and the birds can be heard whistling in the garden. Mary is laying the table with a cloth, and setting out some cups and saucers. She pops outside and returns with a tray with a coffee pot on it, and some bowls. She goes over to the sideboard and pours cereals into two bowls, returning to sit down. George enters,

5 humming a tune, with the *Financial Times* under his arm.

He sits at the table with a cheery morning greeting to Mary.

'Coffee dear?' she asks. George nods and she pours.

'What sort of day have you got, George?'

He puts aside his paper and chats to her about what it will be like at the office. He is

10 a financier who deals in the stock market, has lots of important people as clients, and often has to take them out for lunch. He tells Mary about the lunch he will be going to today, on a luxury boat on the river.

'What about you, dear?' he asks.

Mary tells him that she will potter about in the garden later as the weather looks

15 good, and perhaps visit a neighbour for afternoon tea before Nanny brings the children back from school.

George gets up. Mary then says she would like to pop over to the next village this morning, and whether she can use a car. George tells her to use the Mercedes as the Jaguar is in for a service. He sets off for work.

H Maria Marten or the Murder in the Red Barn (see page 44)

The story of Maria Marten has been told by a number of playwrights. Constance Cox has written a short version, and Brian Burton a full-length play based on the original plays.

Maria Marten was a young girl living with her elderly parents on the estate of a wealthy landowner. William Corder, the son of the landowner, was attracted to her, and eventually
5   lured her away and slept with her. She became pregnant, and he hid her in a cottage away from her parents. He promised he was going to marry her. She foolishly believed him until she discovered that he was engaged to another, wealthy, woman.

Maria had her baby and came back to her home village to try and see William Corder, the villain. Corder kept promising to take her away. Then the baby became sick, and under
10   the pretence of providing medicine, he poisoned it. Worried she is going to cause trouble, he tricks her into going to the Red Barn to meet him at night, where he discovers the baby is dead. When Maria threatens to reveal what has happened unless he marries her, they argue and he shoots her. He buries the bodies of the baby and Maria using a spade borrowed from a country yokel, a friend of Maria's.

15   Maria's parents are worried at her disappearance, and her mother has a dream that features the Red Barn. There is a search and the bodies are found. An officer of the law puts pieces of the puzzle together, and Corder is arrested. He confesses, and eventually expresses remorse for his actions.

There is a sub-plot involving a gypsy whose sister was treated in the same way by Corder,
20   and who sets up the meeting with Maria as bait to try and get vengeance. She assists the police with evidence to catch Corder.

Extracts

A *Happy Home 1* (see pages 23, 30, 46, 47)

John is in his 30s, father of Melissa, who is six. He is out of work. Lydia is also in her 30s and married to John.

This scene takes place in the kitchen of their small house. Melissa is playing at cooking a meal.

	JOHN:	Watch what you are doing!
	MELISSA:	I am, I am.
	JOHN:	You shouldn't be by the cooker.
	LYDIA:	She's all right, John. She hasn't got many places where she
5		can play.
	MELISSA:	Can we go to the park?
	LYDIA:	Not just now.
	MELISSA:	But we haven't been to the park for ages!
	LYDIA:	I'm sorry, but there just isn't time.
10	MELISSA:	Why not?
	JOHN:	Because your mother's getting ready for work.
	MELISSA:	Can't you take me, daddy?
	JOHN:	No. I've got to fill this form in.
	MELISSA:	Why?
15	LYDIA:	Don't bother your daddy, Melissa.
	MELISSA:	But why does he have to do the form now?
	LYDIA:	So he can try and get a job, darling.
	MELISSA:	Well, can't you take me then, mummy?
	JOHN:	Your mother's going to work. We need the money
20		so stop asking.
	LYDIA:	Do I look alright, John?
	JOHN:	You'll do. You're only in reception, not on the catwalk.
	LYDIA:	I know, but you never know, I might catch the boss's eye
		and I might get promoted.
25	JOHN:	He can keep his eyes off you!
	LYDIA:	The 'he' is a 'she', John.
	MELISSA:	Can't I go to the park then?
	LYDIA:	No!
	JOHN:	No!

As they shout at her together, they both turn sharply towards her in anger. Melissa, frightened, jumps up. She has been playing with the cooker. On the top of the cooker is a pan of boiling vegetables. She catches the handle with her arm and knocks it off all over her. She screams.

B *Happy Home 2* (see page 47)

John is in his 30s, father of Melissa, who is six. He is out of work. Lydia is also in her 30s and married to John.

This scene takes place in the kitchen of their small house. Melissa is playing at cooking a meal.

	JOHN:	Watch what you are doing!
	MELISSA:	I am, I am.
	JOHN:	You shouldn't be by the cooker.
	LYDIA:	I wonder if the fridge door will squeak when I open it.
5	MELISSA:	Can we go to the park?
	LYDIA:	The car is very noisy.
	MELISSA:	But we haven't been to the park for ages!
	LYDIA:	I think I might suck a lemon.
	MELISSA:	Why not?
10	JOHN:	What are our cups made out of, china or plastic?
	MELISSA:	Can't you take me, daddy?
	JOHN:	I've got to fill this form in.
	MELISSA:	Why?
	LYDIA:	Don't jump in the water.

C *The Theft* (see page 49)

a PETE: Why are you looking at me like that?
  EMILY: I think you stole the pen.

b PETE: Why are you looking at me like that?
  EMILY: **I** think you stole the pen.

c PETE: Why are you looking at me like that?
  EMILY: I **think** you stole the pen.

d PETE: Why are you looking at me like that?
  EMILY: I think **you** stole the pen.

e PETE: Why are you looking at me like that?
  EMILY: I think you **stole** the pen.

f PETE: Why are you looking at me like that?
  EMILY: I think you stole **the** pen.

g PETE: Why are you looking at me like that?
  EMILY: I think you stole the **pen**.

D *Two's Company* (see page 50)

	PERSON A:	I would like a word with you.
	PERSON B:	What about?
	PERSON A:	I want to know what is going on.
	PERSON B:	What are you on about?
5	PERSON A:	It's no good coming the innocent with me.
	PERSON B:	I really don't know what you are talking about!
	PERSON A:	How could you?
	PERSON B:	Look, I've had just about enough of this.
	PERSON A:	Oh you have, have you?
10	PERSON B:	Yes, and I think you should watch out.
	PERSON B:	Well, I think you are the one who should be watching out!

Introduction for the teacher

Section B of the book contains structures that can be applied to other content. These structures will work with different stimuli or scripts. It is important that students realise this and don't see the structures as content-specific. The students are being given a tool kit, which helps them tackle other drama challenges they work on. This is mentioned in the book, but is more effectively communicated to students if the teacher applies some of the structures in other contexts. The teacher can then draw students' attention to the connections. There is a danger that students think they have to be 'original' all the time, when most of the time they will use tried and tested formulas; the trick is knowing them and selecting when to use them.

Some scripts have been selected that have no copyright, so that schools do not feel they need to purchase play sets. They are also deliberately familiar, as the tasks set can work better with a play the students know already. The focus is not on being absorbed by a new story, but the crafting of a drama pre-text supported by a proactive teacher. The students are approaching the text afresh using their drama eyes, developing their skills as directors, devisers, designers and performers. The teacher will help the students negotiate meaning and create their own 'texts' while also developing understanding of existing plays. This will often involve the teacher as an active participant in the work. This is the case with the *Interactive Museum Structure* based on *Macbeth*, and *The Romeo and Juliet Court Case*.

Introduction for the student

This part of the book contains practical work designed to develop your knowledge and understanding of drama. Each sub-section is self-contained, with enough work to fill half a term or more. However, it is possible to dip into each sub-section, selecting tasks you and your teacher think relevant to you at any particular point in your course. They are set out in a sequence that allows you to build your expertise, but you can change the order to suit the needs and interests of your group. The areas of study and opportunities to work as deviser, designer, director and performer are mixed into all the sub-sections, so you are building your expertise and knowledge throughout the projects. When creating drama you need to combine the areas of study rather than see them as separate entities. The sub-sections have a teaching focus, so in each of them you will be directed through a sequence of work using someone else's ideas and knowledge before being encouraged to use your own ideas. Each sub-section has work that could lead into the creation of a performance piece. The projects you choose to develop in this way are up to you and your teacher. It will not be practical, due to time constraints, for you to develop all the performance suggestions.

B1 Working together – ensemble theatre

This project is placed first, as it is about working as a team, and a drama group needs to learn to operate together and respect each other. You will already have done work with your teacher to encourage this and performing a play together is a great way to cement team spirit.

NOTE TO TEACHERS

This project provides a structure for working on a segment of text and building on it. The format will work with other texts you want to use or adaptations/original scripts you create yourself. Therefore replace the text with a short extract of your own choice and apply the same tasks.

Covering assessment requirements of the course:

- *The project could be used as a means of working on coursework assessment Unit 1, being one of the three scripts required. When you come to do that assessment you could refer back to knowledge gained working on this script or have Unit 1 grow out of this project.*
- *It could likewise provide a basis for coursework assessment Unit 2, being used as the stimulus or theme for the Unit.*

PROJECT SUMMARY

Objective: To work as a whole class to create a piece of **ensemble theatre**.

Purpose: Drama is a social art: you work together as a whole class group or in small groups. Therefore the drama class must become a supportive unit if you are to achieve good results on this course. You must help each other to take drama risks without fear of being mocked or undermined. It's part of becoming '**drama brave**'. Creating a piece of ensemble theatre together is a good way of developing team spirit.

Specification coverage: You will be working with all the areas of study and will have the opportunity to consider the type of problems that need to be solved by deviser, designer, director and performer.

Portfolio: Any record you keep of the unit can contribute to one of the portfolios you have to keep for the exam. However, if you are doing this project early in your course, i.e. in the first two terms, use a working portfolio so you can develop your skills of reflection and record-keeping. This means you can practise these skills and get better at them, so that the portfolios you need to produce for the two coursework Units and the practical exam are your best work.

Information

Ensemble theatre is a specific way of shaping and performing drama. Famous theatre practitioners who have worked in this way include:

- Bertolt Brecht, who founded the Berliner Ensemble in the 1950s, his play *The Caucasian Chalk Circle* adapts very well to the ensemble approach
- Joan Littlewood, who set up the Theatre Workshop in the East End of London, producing a classic ensemble play *Oh What A Lovely War* in the 1960s
- Northern Stage Company, a present day company who have used this dynamic approach to adapt *Animal Farm* and other works.

Later in your course you could look at extracts from these plays with your teacher, or use them in coursework Unit 1, where you have to look at scripts from different genres.

Key features of ensemble theatre

- Deviser, designer, director and performer work together as a team, often over a long period of time (you will be working with your drama group for two years).
- Functions merge, e.g. performers contribute to the script and design, designers contribute to direction, etc.
- The script evolves during the devising and writing process. Writers often work with a company to create the script.
- There are no 'star parts' and often actors play many parts.
- Content is often dealt with in an episodic or broad sweep rather than the format of 'the well-made play' with a clear plot line. The content is often centred on 'big events', e.g. *Oh What A Lovely War* deals with the carnage of the First World War, or sweeping novels, e.g. the Royal Shakespeare Company's adaptation of *Nicholas Nickleby*.
- It can be an ideal way to work with large casts and create exciting 'big group scenes'.
- It makes possible imaginative approaches to setting and communication, with more reliance placed on the resources of the performer rather than technical effects. Songs, music, sounds, symbolism, physical theatre etc. are used to keep a continuous flow of action.
- Design has to be flexible and not necessarily descriptive, i.e. it is not totally realistic or naturalistic. Symbolic or representational design is often used. One large branch symbolises a forest, a flag and rostra represent the battlements of a castle. The main concern is to keep the performance flowing.

Practical work on ensemble theatre

The text below has been adapted from *A Christmas Carol* by Charles Dickens. In the performance you are going to create it is the first scene of the play. (You can take a full version of the play from the website www.heinemann.co.uk/secondary/drama/) As an ensemble you will gradually add to it and make changes as you see fit. However, it is a teaching exercise, so to start with, stick to the suggestions that follow the text on the next page.

Your teacher will be part of the ensemble during the first stages of the project and will take the role of Scrooge. The whole drama class will take the role of Marley's Ghost. At a later stage someone else can play Scrooge.

Remember, as you work on the following tasks, that you can take time out to give each other feedback. This can be done in pairs or groups. You might give advice on acting a role or working on other aspects of the performance.

Preparation tasks

1 Read the script together. One way this can be done is reading it round in a circle. The teacher reads Scrooge, the class read Marley's Ghost to slash marks, with the next student in the circle taking over at each new slash mark. You are reading the text at this stage as explorers or detectives, not performers, so don't be afraid to ask if you don't understand any words. You are a team, so support each other, sharing knowledge and expertise.

Marley's Ghost

SCROOGE:	How now, what do you want with me?
MARLEY:	Much.
SCROOGE:	Who are you?
MARLEY:	Ask me who I was.
5 SCROOGE:	Who were you then?
MARLEY:	In life I was your partner, Jacob Marley. You don't believe in me?
SCROOGE:	I don't.
MARLEY:	Why do you doubt your senses?
	Marley lets out a dreadful cry and there is a rattling of chains.
10 SCROOGE:	Mercy! Dreadful apparition, why do you trouble me?
MARLEY:	Man of worldly mind do you believe me or not?
SCROOGE:	I do, I must, but why do spirits walk the earth and why do they come to me?
MARLEY:	It is required of every man that the spirit within him walk abroad among his fellow men / and travel far and wide; / and if that spirit goes not forth in life it is condemned to do so after death; / it is doomed to wander through the world / and witness what it cannot share, but might have shared on earth, and turned to happiness.
SCROOGE:	You are fettered, tell me why?
20 MARLEY:	I wear the chain I forged in life – / I made it, link / by link, / by link / and yard by yard; / and of my own free will I wore it. / Is its pattern strange to you? / Or would you know the weight and length of the strong coil you bear yourself? / It was full as heavy and as long as this seven Christmas Eves ago. / You have laboured on it, since. / It is a ponderous chain.
SCROOGE:	Old Jacob Marley, tell me more. Speak, comfort me, Jacob.
MARLEY:	I have none to give you Ebenezer Scrooge, that is conveyed by other ministers, to other kinds of men, / I cannot rest, I cannot stay, I cannot linger anywhere. / My spirit never walked beyond our counting-house* / mark me! / – in life my spirit never roved beyond the narrow limits of our money-changing hole; / and weary journeys lie before me!
SCROOGE:	Seven years dead and travelling all the time?
MARLEY:	The whole time / no rest, / no peace, / incessant torture of remorse. / Why did I walk through crowds of fellow beings with my eyes

turned down / and never raise them to that blessed star which led the wise men to a poor abode? / Hear me, my time is nearly gone. / I am here tonight to warn you, that you have yet a chance and hope of escaping my fate. / You will be haunted by three spirits: / without their visits you cannot hope to shun the path I tread. / Expect the first tomorrow when the bell tolls one. / Expect the second on the next night at the same hour / – the third on the next night when the last stroke of 12 has ceased to vibrate. / Look to see me no more. / Remember what has passed between us.

40

45 NARRATOR: The spectre floated out on the bleak dark night and Scrooge, much in need of repose, went straight to bed without undressing and fell asleep upon the instant.

* a counting-house was where money lenders worked from.

2 Stay in a circle and as a whole class group, or splitting into smaller groups of four to six, workshop reading the script as performers. Experiment using different 'vocal atmospheres' by all reading together the same line at the same time, projecting your voice across the circle to the person opposite you. Here are some ideas to get you started:

- in a stage whisper
- speaking slowly, making key words last a long time and using lots of pauses
- declaiming in a very artificial style, like a 'town crier'
- fast, like a sprinter coming out of the blocks.

Try a selection of these and try to tune into the pace and tone of everyone else as you perform. Being sensitive to the pace and pitch of those around you is like playing jazz together and is developing some of the skills you need to be good at drama improvisation.

Development tasks

3 On your own, choose three to five sections of Marley's words that you would love to perform. Choose lines from throughout the script, e.g. some from the beginning, middle and end. Don't necessarily take complete speeches, especially the very long ones. Pick extracts you are going to memorise quickly. The slash marks are a way of breaking the script up for use by a **chorus** of Marleys.

4 Collect together with your teacher and check that all of Marley's words are being covered. A whole group read through will quickly establish any gaps. If there are any lines not being covered, distribute them to volunteers. It doesn't matter if some lines are being spoken by a number of voices and some by one voice. Nor does it necessarily matter if everyone speaks the lines in time, echoing lines can be very effective. Do a final read through to check everyone knows what they're doing and all the lines are covered.

5 It is now time to be 'drama brave' and take your words for a 'walk' around the room. Get used to hearing your voice in the public space and practise different ways of saying the words. Continue to be 'brave' and independent, don't be distracted by anyone else. Finally select how you think it should be spoken. This whole process shouldn't last more than five minutes. .

6 Now go round the room, face the first person you come to and perform your lines to them. This is done simultaneously, both speaking at the same time. Then move on, delivering your lines to as many people as you can get through in a four-minute spell.

7 Now match your voice to your body movement, making sure the two complement each other. Repeat the exercise from task 6 but this time taking turns to deliver the lines. Make sure it is a complete vocal and physical performance.

8 Reflection. Who did you work with who did some quality work? You have two minutes to go and tell them what was special about their performance and you might need to go to more than one person. If you're a 'brave' group with lots of students doing interesting work, you might need more than two minutes!

Performance tasks

9 Perform the scene, remembering the delivery will be ad hoc in that everything hasn't been organised. This is a form of improvisation as, although you all know what you are going to say individually, you haven't organised how you will collectively speak lines. Don't forget what was said above about treating the work like a piece of jazz and that in any improvisation you have to respond to others and sometimes yield. The group is learning to improvise together. It's a bit like getting used to the other players in a football team.

10 Starting point for the scene. The class make the four walls of Scrooge's bedchamber (make it a big room!), stand neutrally heads down or with backs to Scrooge. Place Scrooge in the centre of the room. A chime bar is used to strike midnight. As the bell is struck the walls of the room 'come to life', i.e. the actors representing the walls of the room move in to confront Scrooge and the dialogue begins. The scene will end with the walls of the room being re-formed as the final narrated speech is spoken. As the Marleys 'vaporise' back into the walls, they can echo key words or phrases. Finally, silence and stillness.

11 The scene now has a basic shape and, sticking to the given text, you can work on making it more theatrical. You now need to develop and organise the scene into a cohesive piece of theatre. Decisions need to be made. The key decision is what **genre** are you working in and what **style** of acting will go best with this. If your purpose is to create a really dark and terrifying piece, then everything you do must work with this intention. On the other hand, if you want to create a spoof or **satire** on this material, you must shape it accordingly. Your decision may depend on your chosen audience.

In the rehearsal stage it can be fun to try two contrasting **genres**. The dividing line between **comedy** and **tragedy** can be very fine, but what is different is the attitude of mind of the actor to the performance.

Creating atmosphere that matches chosen genre and style of performance

Consider and experiment with the following, as you think relevant.

- How are you going to move and speak? Those delivering the same lines can plan together if they wish.
- What are you going to add to create your chosen atmosphere? Try adding effects like music, percussion, vocals, and then decide if they help or hinder.
- Consider using lengths of rope or cloth to symbolise chains. Try using them to ensnare Scrooge in a 'spider's web'.
- Experiment with the effect created by using muslin to drape around Marley's body and/or head.
- Experiment with some of you representing furniture in the room. You could ask your teacher to organise a separate physical theatre workshop, experimenting with ways of creating grandfather clocks, chairs, fireplaces, doors etc.

12 Experimentation is over: present the scene as a piece of theatre with full dramatic discipline.

Reflect, discuss and then make a record for your working portfolio

- What have you learnt about working together? List the three key points and say why they are so important.
- What have you learnt about creating a piece of theatre? List three theatrical skills you used.
- Note any other knowledge you have gained about drama or theatre.
- Identify one area you think you need to work on in future lessons to develop your potential in drama.

Developing further scenes to create a short play

As a whole class ensemble you have created the opening scene. Now you will need to split into four working groups and may wish to refer to a copy of the original story to help with the development of your improvised scene. However, it is possible to work with just the information given below.

Group 1: You will improvise the scene of the spectre(s) who come to take Scrooge to his Past, Present and Future. You will be responsible for guiding him to each new scene. How you dramatically create the 'journeys' is for you to decide. You can make a lot of each journey creating a 'ghost world' for him to travel through or do it quickly, moving into the next scene as efficiently as possible.

Suggested key prop: a length of rope/cloth to symbolise chains or threads pulling him to his destiny.

Group 2: You will improvise the scene of The Ghost of Christmas Past. It is essential you communicate that Scrooge was popular and happy at this time of his life; he was in fact engaged to be married. The scene will be set at the Fezziwigs' Christmas party. Remember to try and capture the atmosphere of a different historical time, i.e. Victorian (see picture below).

Suggested key props: a punch bowl, Christmas gifts, cloaks.

A Victorian Christmas in a well-to-do family

Group 3: You will improvise the scene of The Ghost of Christmas Present. The scene is set in the Cratchit's home. It is essential you communicate that Tiny Tim is loved deeply and a favourite of the whole family. The family have just finished Christmas dinner and they await the arrival of the meagre pudding. Bob Cratchit proposes a toast to Scrooge 'the founder of the feast'. Mrs Cratchit is not too thrilled by this, as she thinks Scrooge is a bad employer. Nonetheless, the toast is made. The scene ends ironically with Bob Cratchit drinking the health of someone who treats him so badly.

Suggested key props: Tiny Tim's crutch, a small Christmas pudding.

Group 4: You will improvise the scene of The Ghost of Christmas Yet To Come, which deals with the funerals of both Tiny Tim and Scrooge. It is essential you communicate the sense of loss and grief at Tiny Tim's funeral and the bleak emptiness at Scrooge's. The scene is set in the graveyard, with the funerals taking part in different corners of the cemetery.

Suggested key props: Tiny Tim's crutch, a bible, a tombstone for Scrooge, which can be drawn on sugar paper.

Performance style

Work in the ensemble style of theatre to link the scenes together. Everyone will remain on stage throughout the performance. When not performing, you are around the edges of the performance space, watching or creating sounds or physical images that support the text and add to the atmosphere.

A selection of key properties

Scenario for scene 6

The whole 'company' improvises scene 6 together. Scrooge has been returned to his bedchamber by the spectre(s). The next morning he awakes, goes to the window and opens it. He sees the many smiling faces and enquires what day it is. The crowd are amazed he does not know. They tell him it's Christmas morning. He summons a boy and sends him to buy the prize turkey from the butcher's shop, with the instruction to deliver it to Bob Cratchit's home. Scrooge wishes all those in the street a happy Christmas and a prosperous New Year. The whole cast turns to the audience and wishes them the same season's greetings.

Tip: Preparing this short play could be worked at over four or five lessons. Candidates working towards the practical exam might use it to see what they can produce in ten hours. This is the time you will have to create a performance and prepare a portfolio of evidence in the actual exam. This could be a practice run.

SCENE 1
Marley's Ghost

SCENE 2
Arrival of spectres to collect Scrooge

SCENE 3
Ghost of Christmas Past

SCENE 4
Ghost of Christmas Present

SCENE 5
Ghost of Christmas Yet To Come

SCENE 6
Christmas Day

Information

This version of the play ends in a sentimental fashion, in keeping with many of Dickens's novels. The play could be performed in a melodramatic style, with exaggerated characters and large, over-the-top acting. Dickens loved the theatre and sometimes his novels read like plays. His dialogue can often be lifted straight from the books and acted out with very little adaptation. That is the case with the 'Marley's Ghost' scene you worked on.

However, the scripting and performance style could be much 'darker', in keeping with much of the content. This darker side is evident in much of Dickens's work. In novels like *Nicholas Nickleby* he's like a journalist, exposing the scandal of child cruelty in Yorkshire boarding schools. He's continually drawing attention to some of the unpleasant aspects of Victorian society.

Research

To see how the 'Marley's Ghost' scene you performed was adapted from the original, check back with the novel. Practise your own skills as an adapter for the stage. Ask your teacher to select some extracts from Dickens's novels or any other stories they think relevant and adapt one of them for the stage. Perform it yourself or direct it or give it to another group of actors. This is good practice for work as a deviser, director or performer, one of which you could focus on for your summative task for Unit 1 of your coursework assessment.

Extra task – extending your performance skills

- Perform the scene you created with your small working group in a contrasting genre. For example, if you performed it melodramatically, now perform it as tragedy or in the horror genre etc.
- What are the advantages and disadvantages of each genre you used?
- What audience does each genre best suit?

What have you learned?

This project is designed to help you support and appreciate the work and personality of your fellow drama students. A class with good social health creates high quality work. You have also gained knowledge and developed understanding of the following areas of study.

Character and context

When you created Marley, and whoever else you played in the other scenes, you will have acted out a role. This was not the detailed character work, however, that you will have a chance to explore in later projects.

Structure, shaping and plot

At first you worked with a given structure, but later you shaped your own scenes and improvised around Dickens's original story. You were adapting and adding to a given plot.

Defining performance space

For each scene you worked on, the setting had to be established, as well as entrances, exits and staging.

Improvisation

You were using this core skill throughout the unit as you devised and rehearsed.

Genre, style and conventions

You were asked to choose a genre and performance style to work in. Conventions were not referred to in the unit but you will probably have used conventions such as still image, thought-tracking and hot-seating in the devising and performance work that you did.

The semiotics of drama and theatre

Throughout the shaping and devising you had to consider what you were signalling and how, e.g. using your voice for effect, use of props, defining the performance space.

If you go on to shape the project for performance you will also have covered:

Audience

Who is it for and how does that influence the performance?

PORTFOLIO

You will need to refer to the specification to answer these questions.

- Referring to the content list in the specification, note what skills and knowledge you used from each of the areas of study you covered.

- Look at the assessment objectives and note which parts of the descriptors you achieved.
- What mark would this give you?
- Check this with classmates and your teacher to see if they agree with you.

Practising for the written paper

> Section A questions are designed to be answered on one sheet of A4 in a maximum time of ten minutes.
>
> Section B questions require a maximum time of thirty minutes to answer, using approximately two to three sheets of A4, depending on how much space is used for drawings.

Answer the following questions:

Section A

1 Which theatre genre would you use to perform *A Christmas Carol*? Explain why you have chosen this genre.

2 How did you create atmosphere and meaning in the 'Marley's Ghost' scene?

3 As a director you are required to help the actor preparing to play the role of Scrooge. What advice would you give on the playing of the role?

Section B

1 Make a ground plan (see pages 29–30 for definition and example) of the setting for a performance of *A Christmas Carol*. Explain how you solved the problems of staging the play.

2 a As a costume designer, describe briefly your overall concept (period, style and colour scheme) for the costumes in your drama.

  b Using detailed notes and sketches, show how you would costume two of the characters from your drama. Give reasons for your choices.

3 Write an extended piece of dialogue for two or three of the characters in one of the scenes you devised for the drama.

B2 Working on genre, style and convention

NOTE TO TEACHERS

Covering assessment requirements of the course:

- *The project could be used as a means of working on coursework assessment Unit 1, as examples of scripts for various genres are suggested. These can be dipped into. The Jason and the Argonauts script (see website: www.heinemann.co.uk/secondary/drama/) could be your full text. If you do the Unit 1 assessment at a later stage in your course you could refer back to these texts, using them to make up the three scripts studied. You have a lot of options.*

- *It could provide a basis for coursework assessment Unit 2, being used as the stimulus or theme for the Unit.*

PROJECT SUMMARY

Objective: To develop your understanding and confidence in working with different genres, styles and conventions.

Purpose: To develop understanding of how genre and style offer the possibility of variety in your work, giving alternative ways of communicating to an audience. Within the work you will also have the opportunity to apply dramatic conventions and explore and shape the drama created. This will increase your expertise in the application of dramatic conventions.

Specification coverage: You will be working with all the areas of study at various stages of the project, but there will be emphasis on area of study 6 – genre, style and convention. There will also be opportunities to consider and solve the type of problems that are tackled by deviser, designer, director and performer.

Portfolio: Activities are suggested to help you develop your skills of reflection and enable you to create a high quality portfolio. You and your teacher may have other ideas that you wish to add to the portfolio. Always use your own initiative to extend and develop what is offered in this support book.

Genre and style

A reminder about genre and style is probably helpful at this point, as these terms can cause confusion. You can get into a tricky debate about what is a genre and what is a style, but don't get too worried about being exact with this, as you can't be totally precise. Genre and style merge into each other. In this course, style relates to the performance style selected. The important thing is you learn to use the underlying ideas that make up the concepts of genre and style to create practical drama. Enjoy the new possibilities they add to your work.

Genre can help you organise your drama in a way that makes it connect with an audience. To an extent they know what to expect, i.e. pantomime with its established comic traditions, or melodrama with stock characters such as the wicked villain or the pure heroine. Certain content may suit a specific genre, e.g. **satire** is effective for criticising politicians or social institutions. The most common genres are listed in section A, pages 37–40. You are *not* expected to cover every genre during your course, but you are expected to understand how genre influences the shaping of drama.

Style of performance can be used to match the content of the play or improvisation or to add novelty and create an impact. Some styles you can choose from are listed in section A, page 40–42.

Exaggerated over-the-top acting is a feature of both the pantomime and melodrama genres. However, if you take a common pantomime plot, such as Cinderella, and perform it in a naturalistic style, i.e. as if it were real life, you will be forced to concentrate on the story line and accurate observation. The traditional elements of pantomime such as 'hissing the villain' or 'he's behind you', won't be appropriate. A naturalistic **style** of acting would suit turning Cinderella into a story about a dysfunctional family using the kitchen sink **genre**. The selection of style, genre and plot/theme can be mixed to make very different dramas about the same theme or plot. This is illustrated in the first task below.

'You First Smee!' – a scene from *Who's A Clever Girl*, a pantomime by the Leicestershire Schools Theatre Company

Preparation and exploration tasks

1 Take the story line of Cinderella, making it a story of a boy or girl who has step-parents. Select part of the story, e.g.:

- an invite arrives for a big posh party, the family can't afford for everyone to go;
- Cinderella trying to tell her father how she feels about her stepmother;
- stepsisters making life unpleasant for Cinderella;
- talking to a friend about the problems of your new mother and sisters;
- dreaming of a more romantic life, etc.

Discuss, then split into groups of a number which matches the scenario chosen. If only two characters are needed, then work as a pair. Don't think each scene needs to be different; several groups could work with the same plot. A planning group of four could split into twos for the acting. Perform the scene in a naturalistic style using the kitchen sink genre. If you are successful it should be like something from a soap opera such as *EastEnders*. Spend fifteen to twenty minutes on this.

2 Using the kitchen sink genre again (or, as it is also called, the **slice-of-life** genre) create an improvisation between two or three characters of different ages (Who?), which is set in the living room of a semi-detached house (Where?), in the middle of a weekday afternoon (When?), where there is a problem or tension of some sort (What?). When you plan the scene consider the factors that define a role (see page 9, section A): status, class, beliefs,

personality etc. You are going to work in a naturalistic style again, which means you have to make it as true to life and authentic as possible. Spend a maximum of ten minutes planning the scene, then fifteen minutes improvising it. Remember your challenge is to make it *as accurate and true to life as possible.*

3 Write up your scene as a script, which will be handed to another group for performance. Remember to write it to be performed in a naturalistic style.

Note Writing dialogue is good practice for working as a deviser. This is an option you can take for your summative task in Unit 1 of your coursework assessment.

4 Give the script to another group to perform. As performers you must turn the words on the page into a dynamic performance. If the script is brilliant you've got a head start, if it's not you've got to use your performing and directing skills to make a little piece of magic. Take ten to fifteen minutes to rehearse the scenes, then perform them to each other. The original devisers get to see their 'play' performed.

5 Each group should take a new scene and perform it with an over-the-top style of acting, with the characters as stereotypes. Include the following two features of melodrama: characters step forward to address the audience (this is called an **aside**); one character is portrayed as the 'baddy' and another as a naive victim. You may be able to achieve this by just changing your acting approach; however, you may have to adapt the script. Take fifteen to twenty minutes over this.

6 Make groups of four to six people, take one of the original scenes from task 2 and decide what it's trying to communicate, e.g. Is it about a teenager not being able to communicate with an adult? Is it about love? Is it about fear? Is it about isolation? Write down on a piece of paper a sentence, phrase or word which sums up what the scene is about. This is not the plot, but the essence or 'guts' of the scene.

Your dramatic challenge is to communicate this essence, not in a naturalistic way as in your original script, but in an **abstract** style. Abstract style is a bit like the difference between the paintings of Constable (*The Hay Wain*) and Picasso (*Guernica*) (see page 41 for definition). Don't worry too much about this at the moment, but when you've finished the work suggested, it should be much clearer what is meant by an abstract style.

Some issues that could be included:

- outside pressures the characters face, e.g. at work, at school, with the law
- personal issues, e.g. health, family loyalty, friendship, love.

These issues can be built into the script by:

- using an abstract style and drama conventions such as: **pressure circle, conscience alley, good angel bad angel, freeze frames** etc. (for a reminder of the meaning of these terms, see *Structuring Drama Work*)

- creating a **sound collage** to match the mood or thoughts or fears of a character
- using symbolic props, specific colours of material or light to communicate atmosphere and ideas, e.g. the character feels physically threatened so a red strip of material is wrapped around them by one of the cast as they sink to their knees.

Spend ten minutes planning and fifteen to twenty minutes trying it out.

Do you now understand the difference between an abstract and naturalistic style of drama? Discuss this with your teacher.

These tasks have helped you to start thinking about and exploring genre and style. You will be using conventions as tools for exploration and sometimes performance throughout your course. This is just a start.

TOP TIPS

- Throughout the course, whenever you devise or work with a script, try performing it in at least two styles. It's a fun exercise, but it also helps build performance confidence and helps you develop an insight into how effective using different styles is for communicating ideas dramatically. Content can be viewed with a completely different perspective. Professional actors often do such exercises. When the theatre director Brecht was working on the tragedy *King Lear* he got his actors to perform in a pantomime style in the early rehearsals.

- During the course when you devise scenes, regularly set yourself the challenge of devising using different genres. In the tasks above you used the kitchen sink genre, which is a genre most of you will be familiar and comfortable with. However, you won't be developing your knowledge and drama skills fully if you don't explore the possibilities offered by other genres.

Reflect, discuss and then make a record in your portfolio

- List the genres, styles and conventions you have used so far in this project.
- For each one, state how it was used in your drama.
- State what you think was good about working with this genre, style or convention.
- What types of drama work do you think you might use any of the genres, styles or conventions for in the future?

NOTE TO TEACHERS

Information and development and performance tasks students can tackle during the course, as and when you think appropriate, are noted below. They are best spaced throughout the course, as you don't want to overdose on genre. The tasks will help build knowledge and expertise.

1. Pastiche

Pastiche is a very popular and successful way of working, particularly within the **comedy** genre. Pastiche is like a patchwork quilt of typical material taken from a particular genre. Many television and film comedians take a popular genre and then proceed to lampoon or affectionately send it up. You can send up the horror genre (e.g. the film *Young Frankenstein*), the western genre (the film *Blazing Saddles*) or the disaster movie (the film *Airplane*) or create send-ups of Shakespearean tragedy, war films, musicals, soap operas etc.

Research

Over the next few weeks identify examples of pastiche from television and films you see, and note which genre they are making fun of. Record this for reference in your working portfolio.

Pastiche relies on you being able to identify the standard elements that are used again and again in any genre or, to put it another way, the clichés of the genre. Creating a pastiche from a genre is a very good way of developing your understanding of this part of the course. You can't lampoon or gently poke fun at something successfully unless you understand it.

Four Plays for Coarse Actors and *The Coarse Acting Show 2* have short scripts which send up genres and the theatre generally (see bibliography).

Preparation task

In groups of six or working as a whole class, choose a genre and list on paper (or better still, make still images of) as many clichés relating to the genre as you can think of. Spend twenty minutes on this. This exercise can be repeated for as many genres as you like or for as long as it remains interesting or fun.

> **TOP TIP**
>
> You can repeat the exercise throughout your course as a warm-up activity, which will help you fix in your head what genre is all about. Call it the 'Genre Clichés Game'.

Development and performance task: devise your own pastiche

Choose the genre you want to focus on and create a polished improvisation for presentation to the rest of the group. This will take two to four lessons, depending on how far you wish to develop the work. Your teacher may be able to arrange for you to see video clips of pastiche work. Some of the vintage programmes of comics like Morecambe and Wise and Stanley Baxter are full of excellent examples of pastiche.

2. Satire

This genre is very effective at making fun in a critical way of individuals, groups of people or organisations. Satire can be cruel and hurt people's feelings, as the people on the receiving end of the humour may not always see it as 'only having a laugh'. Satire is never just comedy, but is comedy with a political purpose. Satire can be a way of striking back at powerful people or groups who it is otherwise hard to influence. For instance, using satire to criticise politicians has a long history. Comedians like Rory Bremner work in this way, having a dig at the mighty, rich and famous. *Ubu Roi* is a bizarre play that satirises power and jumped-up officialdom (there is a contemporary update on this play called *King Baabu*).

For satire to work, to make the audience sympathise or think about the observations being made, there must be some truth in the implied criticism. The observations will be distorted and over the top, but they must also be recognisably true. It is the truth of the situation that makes the audience laugh and think. Effective satire doesn't just make you laugh, but makes you annoyed or even angry about some issue or injustice. In order to be truthful the satire has to be based on a topic *you know something about*.

Devise a satirical sketch of your own

What issue in your life experience is worth satirising? It needs to be something that actually matters. You'll have to choose, because for satire to work it has to be based on something important to you and something you have knowledge of. Here are some possible areas to get you thinking.

- Satirise your own age group by looking at how teenagers follow fashion, seek to keep in with the cool group or try not to be seen to work too hard at school.
- Satirise the world of adults and how they relate to young people, or how adults build a false world for young children: the tooth fairy, Father Christmas.
- Satirise teenage anxiety and moodiness, in the vein of Harry Enfield's Kevin and Perry.

Development and performance tasks

1 In working groups, make a list of subjects suitable for satirising. Choose one and devise your sketch. Planning and rehearsing your sketch should take one or two lessons.
2 Perform the sketches to each other.
3 Decide whether you'd like to develop the work for another audience. If the answer is yes, you could put the sketches together to create a **revue**. To get it ready to be performed to an outside audience you will need to **edit**, **adapt**, **add** and **rehearse**. A revue usually has songs and dancing in it. Creating satirical songs and dance routines on your chosen theme could be a challenge and fun. Devising and performing them will extend your drama skills.

Research

Beyond the Fringe was a very famous revue first performed at the Edinburgh Festival Fringe. This revue poked fun at the British establishment in the 1950s, a time of great change in British society. It had a big influence on the development of comedy and satire in this country. The script is published and there are sound recordings of the original cast performing. Reading or listening to some of the sketches will give you an insight into the recent history of comedy in this country. See if you think the material is still relevant and funny.

3. Agitprop

The meaning of this genre is 'agitation' and 'propaganda' and one of its sources was during the Russian Revolution, when plays were presented by revolutionaries to promote their cause and educate the audience (see page 22). This is very much theatre as an 'advertising poster' for your particular cause. The idea is not to present an issue in an even-handed or critical way but to promote your cause and get the audience on your side. It is not such a common genre in this country as it was during the first half of the twentieth century, when there was more social and economic turmoil. A famous example of this genre is the American play *Waiting for Lefty* by Clifford Odets (1934), which has as its theme the New York taxi drivers' strike of that year. In Britain during the miners' strike of 1984–5 a number of theatre companies toured the coalfields performing plays promoting the miners' cause.

Agitprop developed its own distinctive performance style using sketches, cabaret and mime. Setting was minimal, actors dressed in dungarees and the audience was encouraged to participate. Companies composed their own music and songs to fit their themes. Unity Theatre Company, which was a British group, had a big hit song with one of their tunes 'Sing a Song of Social Significance'.

'The Enemy is at the Gates!' Russians are urged to resist the enemies of the revolution, 1919

Preparation tasks

1 In working groups of up to six, pick an issue you feel strongly about. You should select your working group according to the issue you choose – you all need to support the stance you are going to take on the issue. Possible issues include fox hunting; sweat shop or child labour; capital punishment; homelessness; nuclear weapons; road protests; genetically modified crops; school rules etc.

2 Make six still images which promote your cause. They should be like posters promoting your viewpoint, and each should have a caption, which will be

spoken to accompany the image. You have twenty minutes to do this. (Later you could develop this by putting the captions on a cassette tape and adding musical links or songs, raps and poems to go between each image.)

3   When the time is up, every group performs at the same time, running the sequence as if quick changes on a slide projector. Someone calls the numbers 1-6 and you make the images and speak the caption lines. This is a test in group organisation and co-operation. A successful group will be able to do this with no discussion and no fuss. You can now look at each group individually if you think this is important.

Development and performance tasks

1   The images have helped you plan a drama. Follow this up by creating the drama, linking the images together with movement, dialogue, narration, songs, raps, poems etc. You are turning it into a play. Rehearse, edit, adapt and add to create a quality drama. This could take two to four lessons. When complete, decide whether you wish to perform the work to an outside audience, e.g. school assembly.

2   Using the sketch *Art is a Weapon* (1931), which you can find on the Internet at www.heinemann.co.uk/secondary/drama/, rehearse and perform in the style of the political theatre groups. You can achieve this using what you have been told in this section of the book and the clues that the script gives you.

If you are interested in researching further, use the Internet. There is also a book you could refer to: *Theatres of the Left* (Raphael, MacColl, Cosgrove: see bibliography).

Research

The folk songs of American Woodie Guthrie and Britain's Ewan MacColl and Peggy Seeger are very political. Ewan MacColl wrote many songs for the theatre, particularly during his collaboration with the theatre director Joan Littlewood. The popular music scene also has its political songwriters, e.g. Bob Dylan, John Lennon (after he split from the Beatles) and Billy Bragg. Which recent and current pop groups or solo artists do you know of who have produced songs with political lyrics?

TOP TIPS

Use songs, raps and poems in your drama. They are excellent devices for making a commentary on the action – they draw the attention of the audience to the points you are making or give a viewpoint on a character or incident in the drama. A poem can be used to make a point or move the plot on more quickly than conventional scripting. Agitprop and music hall commonly used such devices and they are now used in all forms of theatre.

Breaking into song or using music is conventionally used for moments of heightened emotion. These are the moments when words are not enough, e.g. love and death scenes. They are also tricky moments to act, so putting music on or breaking into song can be a solution!

4. Living newspaper

This is a form of agitprop that has virtually disappeared in this country. Hot political news items were turned into theatre and taken onto the streets as the events were still unwinding. The idea was to make people think and be confronted by these issues on the streets. Often the play would stop in full flow and a debate take place with the audience. This didn't matter in the eyes of the actors, as their aim was to get people thinking about the issue rather than just entertain them. When this type of theatre was popular, during the first half of the twentieth century, there were more people who couldn't read. The drama used the agitprop style, political satire, songs, music and action.

Here is a task in which you could try to put some life into the old format.

Preparation task

Choose a national, local or school news item and turn it into a sketch. The sketch must have a point of view, which you are trying to push. Plan this activity ahead for a set day, so you can bring in papers, school bulletins or other material that could start you off. It must all be hot off the press, so you've got to select the theme there and then on the day. Have one or two practice goes, so you get used to devising and performing a sketch in one lesson.

Development and performance task

Now do it for real, taking the sketch you devise in the lesson out onto the 'streets' of the school the same day as it was devised. It can be performed in the playground, the hall, to the tuck shop queue etc. As you are not in Russia during the revolution, make sure you clear the project with the school head to ensure you are not being a nuisance or creating a health and safety risk. Repeat with a new story on another day. The school gets used to its daily 'living newspaper'.

5. Documentary theatre

(See page 21, section A for definition.)
Context: Evacuation in the Second World War and the Home Front.

Preparation

- Research is needed to provide the factual documentary material, which will then be woven into your drama. The factual material is added as: narration; voiceover; songs; actual recordings of speeches or music from the time; newsflashes; depictions of historical characters or events etc. Collect your resource material from the Internet or your school history department. Beware, there is a lot of information on this subject! The material on page 80 should be enough to get you started.
- The novel *Carrie's War* by Nina Bawden deals with the childhood memories of Carrie, who was evacuated as a child with her brother Nick. There is a stage adaptation which will provide ideas for dramatisation, or you could select extracts from it (see bibliography).

Source material: historical information

1939	
June–September	Evacuation of three and a half million people from the cities. Gas masks issued.
3 September	Declaration of Second World War. Introduction of National Service Act.
December	By the end of the year, 43,000 women in either the Women's Services or nursing.
1940	
January	Start of rationing (butter, bacon, sugar).
March	Meat rationing.
Spring	Women bus conductresses now a common sight.
July	Tea, margarine and other fats rationed. Free or subsidised milk available to mothers. Over 50% of men aged 20–25 in the armed services (over 20% of the total male population).
September	London Blitz begins, which was the most intense period of the London bombing. Nearly one and a half million Londoners (1 in 6) made homeless between September 1940 and May 1941.
1941	
February	1,370,000 officially billeted evacuees.
April	Women's Services became part of the Armed Forces. By June 100,000 women in the Services.
10 May	Last and worst night of the London Blitz.
June	By 19 June: 2 million houses destroyed or damaged: 60% of London. The beginning of clothes rationing. Cheese, eggs and preserves added to the food being rationed.
Summer	Start of Lend Lease food supplies from USA.
December	Full conscription of women. Unmarried women between 20 and 30 years of age subject to call-up. The choice was between the Forces and important jobs in industry (e.g. munitions). Vitamin welfare scheme for children – cod liver oil and then orange juice.
By the end of 1941	The following proportions of women were either at work or in uniform: 80% of single women aged 14–59 years 41% of wives and widows 13% of mothers with children under 14 years.
1942	
February	Increased austerity measures – no petrol for private use, clothes rationing allowance cut. Food rationing extended to include dried fruit, rice, pulses, condensed milk, breakfast cereals, syrup and treacle, biscuits, sweets and soap.

TOP TIP

You don't need too much material to get started. The key is to select material that sparks off drama ideas or supports the ideas you already have.

Development tasks

Select five potential scenarios for development, perhaps from the following.

- An air raid with a family in their Anderson shelter.
- A bombed street: rescue services, relatives and neighbours deal with the aftermath.
- A meeting of parents with a Ministry of Health official at the local school to consider evacuating their children. Your teacher could play the official. Information for the role, plus other valuable resources for this topic, can be found in the resource book *Evacuees* (referred to on page 105 and bibliography).
- In pairs, a parent taking final leave of their child at the station. The parent gives the child their advice, love and one final special keepsake to take with them.
- An evacuee being hawked round the village to be placed with a host family.
- The new school: city evacuees mixing with the country kids.

Around these scenarios the 'documentary commentary' is woven. The purpose is to heighten the meaning and add emphasis to the work. It emphasises that this actually happened to real people. The genre mixes factual material and your drama speculation. Your scenes speculate as to how people might have felt and behaved in those situations.

Select the potential audience you would like to focus the drama for, edit, adapt and add.

Performance task

- If you are to perform this drama you need to consider a possible audience (of course you may have already done this). It might be ideal for a primary school or a group in your own school that is studying this subject.
- Rehearse, edit, adapt, add as necessary.
- Review the final outcome.

NOTE TO TEACHERS

Other genres

If you would like the class to do work on melodrama *or* commedia dell'arte *see the relevant sections in* Progression in Secondary Drama. *The information and practical tasks fulfil the requirements of this course very well.*

Remember, examples of genre given in the specification content are just that, examples. There are others you can use. There follows a genre not listed in the content that you can use for an extended performance project. It could provide the basis for coursework assessment Unit 1 or Unit 2.

6. Fantasy/adventure genre: extended project

If your class tackles the full project you might need up to half a term to complete it. However, you can profitably tackle the opening tasks without going on to create a full-scale performance. Each of the tasks is self-contained so any you tackle will be developing knowledge and skills relevant to your course.

PROJECT SUMMARY

Objective: To devise or perform a drama from the myth *Jason and the Argonauts.*

The story is a **fantasy/adventure** genre. You could target any audience, but this content and genre might suit the top primary to lower secondary school age range. Therefore you could work in a **theatre-in-education** way and make it a **participatory play** whereby you involve the pupils in drama activities and role play. Or you can perform a play which they watch as a traditional audience. Or you could mix the two. Whichever option you take, first do the preparation tasks below.

Source material: There are many versions of the story available. A simplified children's version will give you the basic story, which is all you need. You won't be able to dramatise the

complete story; the skill of the deviser is to select what will make good drama. A very good version of the story is listed in the bibliography.

or

Take the *Jason and the Argonauts* script off the website (www.heinemann.co.uk/secondary/drama) and work as performers, directors and designers with a given script. The script was devised by students with their teacher and is work in progress, so there is a chance for you to add, adapt and edit the play. There is the 1963 film and also a recent television adaptation available on video and DVD (see bibliography).

Performance style: Physical theatre performed by an ensemble.

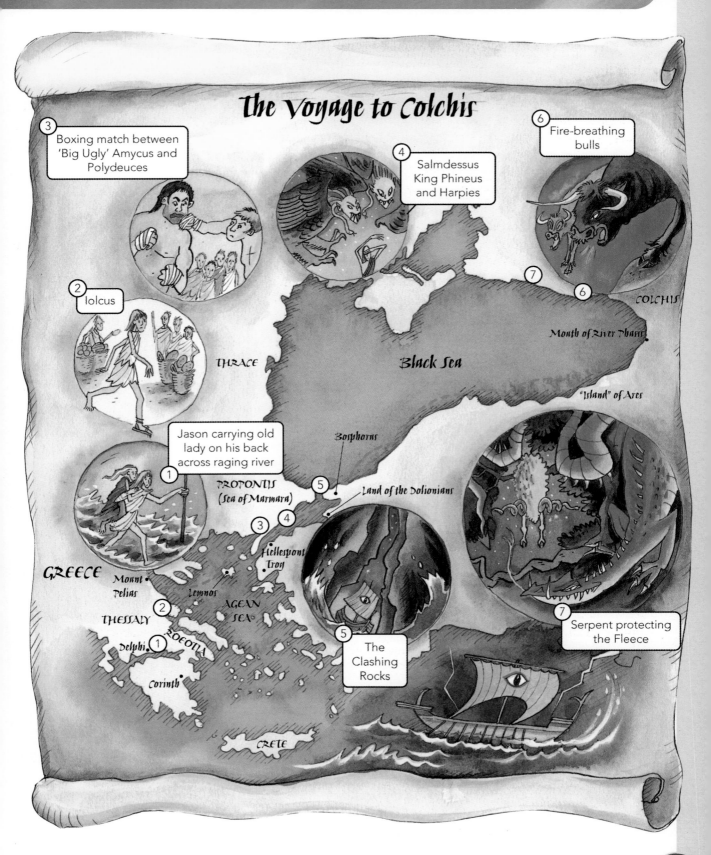

The Voyage to Colchis

3 Boxing match between 'Big Ugly' Amycus and Polydeuces

4 Salmdessus King Phineus and Harpies

6 Fire-breathing bulls

2 Iolcus

1 Jason carrying old lady on his back across raging river

THRACE

Black Sea

COLCHIS

Mouth of River Phasis

7

6

"Island" of Ares

Bosphorus

PROPONTIS (Sea of Marmara)

5 Land of the Dolionians

3

4

Hellespont

Troy

GREECE

Mount Pelias

Lemnos

AEGEAN SEA

THESSALY

BOEOTIA

Delphi

1

2

5 The Clashing Rocks

7 Serpent protecting the Fleece

Corinth

CRETE

Information

A note about the website script. It was written to be acted by an ensemble, using physical theatre as the style for performance (actors physically create the shape of the boat on which the Argonauts sail, the serpent that guards the Fleece etc.). None of the actors left the stage, they were grouped around the edge of the stage watching the action or adding effects/atmosphere at selected points in the script. Costume was a basic black top and bottom to which were added extras such as cloaks, head dresses, sashes etc., as different characters were played. A group of ten Argonauts remained constant and donned red bandannas when they agreed to join Jason on the quest. In this production all the changes were done on stage in full view of the audience – the audience knows it's a play so it doesn't matter if they see the 'nuts and bolts' of the theatre craft. In fact it can be enjoyable to see this. This is working in a way made popular by the theatre practitioner Brecht (see page 23).

The map on page 83 is an elaboration of a prop used for the performance. Features of the fantasy/adventure genre are: the fantastic; jostling between good and evil; eventual redemption; the holders of knowledge; challenges to be met. *The Wizard of Oz* is an example of the fantasy genre and the *Star Wars* films have many elements of it.

Preparation tasks

1 In groups of four or five, each take a different location from the map. Write an imaginary description of your location, working in the fantasy genre. You can mention dangers or characters if you wish, but this is a piece of narration that establishes location and creates an atmosphere for the audience. Take ten to fifteen minutes for this task.

2 Experiment with speaking your narration aloud as a chorus. What tone of voice suits? Where are you going to put the emphasis? Are you all going to speak some parts and use single voices for others? How are you going to stand, as neutral narrators or as characters? Spend ten minutes rehearsing.

3 Each group takes their position in the classroom/studio. Your teacher is an Argonaut and as she/he moves to each location, that group makes a still image then comes to life and speaks their narration. Your teacher will react as they feel appropriate. This process continues until each location has been visited.

You have been working as devisers to create **narration** and as performers to communicate to an Audience. Rather than have a single narrator you have used a **chorus**. The chorus is a very flexible theatrical device. You can use it to: establish a setting; give the audience background detail; create a versatile band of actors who can play a number of roles; provide vocal variety when lengthy sections of 'information' have to be communicated to an audience; sing or create physical imagery to support the text.

Narration is a quick way to create settings. In the case of the map task it emphasised location, but it could equally well be used for:

- historical background to a scene: 'Jason was the son of Aeson, the rightful king of Iolcus. From the moment he was born he was in terrible danger ...'
- time and place: 'It's midnight, the time Jason had arranged to meet Medusa at the temple of Hera. Could he trust the daughter of Aites to help him in his quest for the Golden Fleece?'
- power: 'Pelias was king of Iolcus. He was ruthless and ruled the kingdom by fear and oppression ...'

Development tasks

4   In your working groups create three new pieces of narration for the 'Jason' story. Make them fulfil the same functions as above: historical background; time and place; power. You will need to use a copy of the story to select your content. To devise and perform the narration will take two lessons. Remember, narration needs to be performed just as vigorously and imaginatively as character work. You are storytellers and you must engage your audience. You can choose to rely on the power of the writing and good vocal delivery or you could add physical imagery, which support the narration. You need to experiment and then make your own decisions.

5   In the story of Jason, he and the Argonauts have to overcome various obstacles, e.g. the Harpies, the clashing rocks, the fire-breathing bulls at the Field of Ares, taking the Golden Fleece from the serpent. In working groups experiment on how you could dramatise these events: it could be a mixture of dialogue, movement, narration, song. (Refer to the script on the website to see how it was done there if you wish.) Spend a lesson, possibly two, working on this, then each group takes it in turns to work with the whole class directing them as an ensemble through their scene. Each scene could take up to a lesson to recreate with the whole class.

Performance task

6   You have created some narration and some potential scenes. Piece this together to form your script and edit out any bits you no longer wish to use. Decide what needs to be adapted and what additions need to be made. You need to devise the rest of the play and rehearse it. Good luck with the performance.

What parts of the specification have you covered?

Creating your own script of *Jason and the Argonauts*, or using the one provided, gave you the opportunity to broaden your use of genre, style and conventions (area of study 6).

You have covered working with the fantasy/adventure genre and performed using physical theatre as a style for presentation.

PORTFOLIO

- List three advantages of working with the physical theatre performance style.
- What did you think was the strongest part of the drama/play you created or performed?
- Who impressed you with the work they did on the project a) as a deviser b) as a director c) as a performer d) as a designer?
- List any conventions you worked with and explain how they were used for both the devising process and possibly the final performance.
- What audiences do you think the fantasy/adventure genre is suited to?

Practising for the written paper

(Instructions for answering these questions can be found on page 70.)

Section A

1 Write a dialogue for two characters from one of the 'kitchen sink genre' dramas you created. What is the function of the dialogue in the drama?

2 Write a monologue for one of the characters you created in your work on the satire genre. Give acting directions to make it clear how the actor would deliver this speech to match satire genre.

3 Write a rap or poem that could be used with the drama you created in the agitprop genre. Explain the point you are trying to make.

Section B

1 How did you explore, develop and shape the drama you developed in satire genre (or pastiche or agitprop or documentary)? Include choices you made regarding structuring, plot, genre, performance style and conventions. Give reasons for the choices you made.

2 How would you present the drama you developed in satire genre (or pastiche or agitprop or documentary)? Include genre and performance style, design, performance space and target audience. Justify the choices you make.

3 Outline the plan for a documentary drama you created by listing scenes and any documentary material or links you included. Take one scene plus the links into and out of it and, in detail, explain how it was realised as a practical workable drama.

B3 Working on structure, shaping and plot

PROJECT SUMMARY

There is no one standard format for creating drama; in many ways the rule is: rules are there to be broken. However, it helps to know the rules before you decide when to adapt them or break them.

Objective: To introduce some of the less commonly used formats which are used to organise and shape dramatic action.

Purpose: To give you more options in your drama work and point out there are standard structures you can use to make your dramas. This is often what professional playwrights do. It is not so dependent on being original as you may think.

Specification coverage: You will be working with all the areas of study, but there will be particular emphasis on structure, shaping and plot. You will also be encouraged to explore the type of task and problems faced by deviser, designer, director and performer.

Portfolio: Tasks are included to develop your skills of reflection and to help you practise recording skills in a working portfolio or to create one of the actual portfolios you have to put together for the examination.

Making a start on your own text

When you plan and make your own improvised dramas the five Ws provide a good basis for getting things going – the essential ingredients of any text. This is a basic way of structuring your drama; a range of other ways were introduced in section A, pages 15–17.

When? The time the scene is set in: present, past, future or limbo? The time of day: midnight, dawn?

Where? The location of the scene: a living room, a foggy moor, a city estate?

Who? What characters are involved, what is their personal relationship to each other, and what is the power relationship?

Why? A scene can serve a number of purposes: is the situation or plot being developed; is it introducing us to the characters and situation; is it developing character; is it creating a conflict or dilemma or tension; is it setting an atmosphere; is it moving the plot forward; is it making a statement?

What? What's up? What is the issue of the scene, the problem, the actual guts of the scene?

Preparation tasks – create your own text

Working in groups of three or four.

1 On a sheet of paper create a brief plan for an improvised scene covering the five Ws above. Take five minutes over this.

2 Swap sheets with another group. Your task is to work with each other's plans and create an engaging piece of drama. Take fifteen minutes over this.

3 Perform the scenes for each other.

4 Bring the two groups together to give each other feedback about the original plan and how it was eventually performed.

5 You could now work together on one of the scenes or create each scene in turn, one group acting and the other directing. It can be interesting to change it around a little by letting the original creators of the plan be the actors.

Mixing the functions around is all good practice, working as deviser, director and performer.

TOP TIPS

Repeat this sequence of tasks regularly throughout your course. As you become more skilled, your plans will offer increasing potential for the creation of quality drama. As devisers you will want to give the actors something to get their teeth into. It is also good practice for candidates taking the written paper option, as scripting and writing in role are standard questions.

You can vary the way you set out the plans and by so doing develop your expertise in structuring drama. Here are some ways you can vary the plans.

• Give the scene a clear **climax**, a moment when things come to a head.

• Create a plan with a twist in the plot (**peripetia**).

• Give the plan an **obligatory moment**: something the audience would expect in a drama on this topic. For example, can you have a drama on Henry VIII without dealing with the beheading of his wives?

• The bullet points above are all facets of the **Aristotelian model** (see page 15). You could be more ambitious and plan a longer drama where you try the full model; i) exposition ii) rising action iii) climax iv) denouement. You don't necessarily have to create lots of scenes, you could use the Greek unities of time, place and action (see page 96, Top Tips).

• Create plans for particular types of scenes, e.g. historical, love, horror.

Discuss: What genre and style did you use for your scenes? What did this add to your work? What did you like about working in this way?

Like most GCSE students, you will probably favour structuring and plotting in a naturalistic way, usually working in variations of the kitchen sink genre. This is because this relates to the type of drama most students have commonly experienced. As drama students you will regularly use various dramatic conventions in your work. This adds an abstract element to the work and slows the action down so the implications of important moments can be noted.

There is nothing wrong with this and quality work can be produced as effectively in this way as in any other. The rest of this sub-section concentrates on ways of working you may not be so familiar with. The examples used are drawn from the specification content, explained in section A, page 14–17.

The work here won't cover all that content and it is important to remember you are not expected to cover all the different examples listed – you haven't the time to do this. What is expected is that you will try a minimum of two different formats and understand how these formats for structuring and shaping influence the final drama. It is part of the process of extending your dramatic vocabulary and therefore your dramatic options.

Dramatic metaphor, analogy and allegory

Dramatic metaphor, analogy and allegory all operate by not addressing their theme directly. Working in these ways affects the way you shape your drama, how it looks and the way the plot is organised. As with many issues in the arts, things aren't always straightforward, there aren't simple right or wrong answers. You could debate and argue about whether a play is an allegory or an analogy or whether they are the same thing – even whether these formats are genres or styles.

Remember, in this course, debate over definitions is not as important as the ability to turn the ideas they sparked off in your head into effective drama. Effective drama communicates to an audience, so these concepts are only going to be useful if they help make the dramas you create and interpret more meaningful and engaging for you and an audience. As Shakespeare wrote, *A rose by any other name would smell as sweet.*

A **metaphor** can be created to give an overall unity in a drama, e.g. a character's life story created as a journey with all the various twists and turns.

An **analogy** is used to create a similar situation in a different context, which helps understanding of difficult or sensitive issues. Many fairy stories have an underlying theme 'buried' beneath the surface of the basic plot – they have a **sub-text**.

A few years ago I worked with a group of Israeli Jews and Arabs and the purpose of the drama was to get them talking about the conflict in their country. The aspect of the conflict I chose to explore was 'who owns the land'.

This was much too sensitive an issue to tackle head on in 'now time', i.e. as themselves. I decided to use analogy and approach the issue through a similar historical situation. I chose to work on a drama about Native Americans and white pioneers. The drama dealt with the conflicting claims of these peoples for the land. As the drama progressed the group began making their own connections and comparisons to the Arab/Israeli conflict. The drama about America in the nineteenth century had created a bridge into this very hot issue for the participants.

Allegory deals with its theme symbolically. *Animal Farm*, taken at face value, is about farm animals taking over from their human masters, but it is also a political satire on the Soviet Union following the Russian Revolution. Many fables are allegories, e.g. *Aesop's Fables*. In section A, pages 10 and 52, you can read about the play *Everyman*, one of the theatre's most famous allegorical plays.

Why should playwrights and performers want to work in these ways? Isn't acting out the story as true to life (naturalism) going to be the best way of communicating your ideas? The answer to the last question is, not necessarily. Strict naturalism is not always the best way to expose or reveal the truth of a situation. Below are three reasons why you might choose to work in a less naturalistic way.

1 By performing the drama in an unusual or novel way you might grab the attention of the audience more effectively.

2 The truth of human situations and conflicts is complicated and the reality of the situation may be best created by not making the scene so true to life (naturalistic), e.g. flashbacks can emphasise the history of the situation; voice-overs can tell the audience what is going on in a character's mind; sound collage or music can create the emotional state of mind of a character.

3 In countries where there is no freedom of speech, it may be necessary to criticise the rulers through allegory. The popular story *Gulliver's Travels* was originally a political allegory, which attacked powerful people the author couldn't speak out against directly.

Devising a dramatic metaphor, analogy or allegory to create a context for the whole drama has more to it than including conventions such as flashbacks or voice-overs to a naturalistic plot line.

Discuss: Think of two issues that might make people in the area where you live feel uncomfortable if you dealt with them head on. Try and think of a dramatic analogy, metaphor or allegory that might enable you to explore the issue. Not every situation can be approached through these means, so don't be surprised if you find this hard or can't easily create a parallel. Share your ideas with the rest of the class. If you think the ideas have potential, they could be used to create practical work.

Development and performance tasks

Each of the following seven tasks can take from one to three lessons each. It depends how much detail you go into and whether you decide to polish them for performance or leave them as improvisations. You can select with your teacher how many of the tasks to do and decide whether to do them as a continuous block or intersperse them throughout your course. Portfolio ideas for these tasks are on page 93.

1 Take one of Aesop's many allegorical fables (see bibliography) and turn it into a naturalistic contemporary drama. The process of tackling such a conversion really helps you understand how allegory works and is a drama challenge. Some suggested fables are: *The Four Oxen and the Lion* (the theme is unity is strength); *The Farmer and the Stork* (if you keep bad company you will be treated with suspicion however honest you may be); *The Peacock and the Crane* (judge people by what they achieve not by outward appearance). You must ensure the original point of the allegory is maintained in the new naturalistic drama, so the first thing to do is to establish what the fable is actually getting at.

2 Fairy stories such as *Little Red Riding Hood* can be seen as analogies, i.e. a story about a girl's arrival into womanhood and the 'predators' that await her. You could take a fairy story and explore any 'hidden meaning' or sub-text within it. Give the new version a title, e.g. *The Uncensored Red Riding Hood*. As well as working on analogy you can extend the plots and themes, e.g. *The Three Little Pigs* could focus on why three youngsters leave home and be titled *Leaving Home*. *The Pied Piper* could be titled *The Corrupt Councillors*.

   Note: For a fuller drama project developing some of these ideas see page 120, *The True Story of the Three Little Pigs*.

3 Metaphor is more commonly used in drama classes than either analogy or allegory. Try taking the format of a chess game and use it to show how characters can be manipulated by forces over which they have no control. Or create some other context using the dramatic metaphor of the chess game.

   Example: One drama group created a giant chess board, placing four characters in squares, controlled by two chess players sitting on a raised platform. The students were working in an abstract style to explore their theme. Other students worked with this metaphor in a naturalistic way, two characters playing chess talking about a conflict between them, the chess game serving to emphasise and punctuate their differences. The chess game metaphor can be used in many contexts.

4 Use the format of a game of pool, with two characters sparring to see who can gain the most status with the peer group. Split into pairs to do this and choose something people of your own age might 'compete' over. Each shot will be about the vying personalities rather than the pool game. You'll be working in a naturalistic setting and style, but the pool game becomes a metaphor for something else.

Discuss: Sport is often used in drama as a metaphor, particularly boxing and baseball. Why do you think these sports are used repeatedly and the majority of others rarely?

NOTE TO TEACHERS

The film **The Hustler** *has pool as the background against which the drama unfolds, but it is not essentially a film about pool. The game is a metaphor for the life of its main character,* *Eddy Felson. If you get a copy of this film it is worth watching some clips showing the pool games. What are they telling you about Eddy? It is also a good example of Method acting.*

5 Use chairs to create the setting for a lift. The lift is a metaphor for the different possibilities that life offers the principal character. You could use a character you have created in a previous drama, or a convention such as **role on the wall** to create a new character. Each floor the character alights at offers different possibilities; each can have a different 'master of ceremonies' or you can have one actor controlling all the floors. The lift, like life, goes up and down. The metaphor of the lift gives an abstract style to the overall shaping of the scene, but the scenes you create for each floor can be performed in any style you wish, e.g. naturalistic, non-naturalistic, abstract, representational. It is possible to mix styles and adapt or change the rules.

Example: One drama group used each floor as a different dream world, exploring the character's aspirations and fears. They were working in the **fantasy genre** and used an **abstract style** for performance.

6 Create a pathway or highway representing a journey through life. The character you create or select will encounter obstacles, diversions, accidents and junctions, which all have to be negotiated. You can develop this into quite an elaborate drama, using improvisation and adding conventions such as **monologue**, **still image with captions** and **dialogues** to mark the significant moments on life's journey. The structure of life's journey to shape a drama or story is a classic format, e.g. *Pilgrim's Progress*.

7 Create a wheel of fortune in a fairground. The barker cries 'Round and round she goes, where she lands no one knows. Your fate relies on one little spin of the wheel of fortune. Come forward, lady, your destiny awaits.' The pointer is spun to the accompaniment of fairground music. It stops. What is the fate of the subject of the drama? That is up to you to decide. If you are to work with this dramatic metaphor the theme of the drama might be the fickleness of fate.

Link to work with published scripts

- For either the lift or the pathway you could choose a character from a play you have worked on, e.g. Macbeth or Juliet, and create their pathway through the play. You select from the plot junctions, crossroads, dead ends etc. You could do this for any published text. Select a character and create the lift or pathway metaphor for them. An alternative is to split into four or five working groups, each group choosing a different character from the play. Share the outcomes with each other.

- The play script of *Animal Farm* is a good example of an allegorical play. You could use this text with your teacher and get a good idea of how allegory works. It could be one of the three texts you choose to refer to as a requirement for Unit 1 of your coursework.

PORTFOLIO

The following can be used for any of the seven tasks above.

- List three advantages of working in this way (relate this to any of the specific tasks).

- List one drama situation (context) you think you might use dramatic metaphor, analogy or allegory for. Explain why.

- List any other dramatic metaphors, analogies or allegories you have used in your drama work.

Practising for the written paper

(Instructions for answering these questions can be found on page 70.)

Section A

1 What style of acting did you choose for your drama? List three reasons why this suited your drama.

2 List two ways the idea of dramatic metaphor (or analogy or allegory) was used to shape the drama you created.

3 Outline a plan you made for one of the dramas you devised (What? Who? Why? Where? When?).

Section B

1 How did you explore, develop and shape the drama on metaphor (or analogy or allegory)? Include choices you made regarding structuring, plot, genres, styles and conventions. Give clear reasons for the choices you make.

2 How would you present the drama you worked on for performance? Include genre and performance style, design, performance space and target audience. Justify the choices you make.

3 Explain your overall design concept for your drama. Choose one area from: staging; costume; make-up; lighting; or properties and give details of your designs for this element (use sketches, notes etc. as relevant).

An extended task on dramatic metaphor

This could be a twenty-hour coursework Unit for your assessment or if you are taking the practical exam (realisation test) it could be used as a 'mock' for the final test.

Working as a whole class use the pathway or journey metaphor to create your own play.

Use role on the wall or, better still, an item of costume or artefact as the starting point, e.g. a pair of shoes or jacket to create a character. Someone from the group can volunteer to collect together the starting stimulus or you can ask your teacher to create it. Look at the factors you considered on page 9 (status, personality etc.) and add them to the equation.

You are going to map out the journey through life of the character you create on a large piece of sugar paper.

Preparation tasks

1 Draw the starting line. The starting line can be any point in their life. Using forum theatre, create a still image, which fixes a common drama moment for everyone. The still image will fix the **Where** and **When**, maybe even a hint of the **What**. You can add any characters you think relevant.

2 The journey begins. Are you travelling forwards or backwards? Or a bit of both? The last group I saw do this decided to have 'mostly the past with just a little bit of the future'. There are going to be five key points on the journey: a crossroads; an accident; a bridge; a tunnel; and a brick wall. The full journey, your play, will have five scenes, one for each of these settings. Mark each key point/scene on your route map. What order should they be in? If the brick wall ends the play, does that make the play less hopeful than ending with a bridge? Ending with the brick wall might fix the genre as tragedy. Once you have mapped in the five scenes and put them in order, you are ready to create the full drama.

3 You are going to work as an ensemble so the play needs a unified style for both shaping and design. First try the approach suggested here, which you can review and alter if you don't think it suits your play. Look at the stage ground plan opposite and set up the performance space as shown. Any extras should be kept to a minimum and must be moved on and off the performance space as needed. This must not interrupt the flow of the play, so must be capable of being brought on and off efficiently. When not performing, actors will surround the performance space.

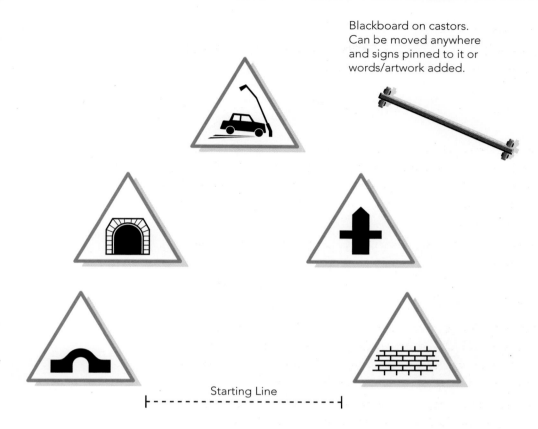

Blackboard on castors.
Can be moved anywhere
and signs pinned to it or
words/artwork added.

Starting Line

Development tasks

4 Split into five working groups and each take one of the scenes. Your scenario should match the metaphor you are working with. So, if you're working with the crossroads, the scene you create is a crossroads in that character's life. The way you devise must also match the performance space and the ensemble way of working. Should the scenes be naturalistic, abstract or a mixture? Fix a time limit and set to work.

5 When the group scenes are completed, you will probably have five different people playing the main character. As a whole class, decide how to signal this to an audience, e.g. do you pass on a prop or piece of costume to signal your 'passing the baton' on to another actor? Do you need a narrator to lead the audience through the journey and link the scenes? In your first run through your teacher could improvise this role.

Performance tasks

6 Perform the play.

7 Split into two groups, one group write a **prologue** for the play, the other the **epilogue**. Perform again.

8 Reflect on the performance. Did it go well? Was it an interesting way of devising and staging a play? If you decide to perform to an outside audience this will involve consideration of editing, adapting, adding and rehearsing.

Developing it further

The same format used for the pathway drama could be applied to the 'lift' or 'wheel of fortune' metaphors. Working groups could be formed as follows:

The lift	Floor 1	The past
	Floor 2	Dreams for the future
	Floor 3	The present
	Floor 4	A happy or unhappy memory
	Floor 5	The future

The wheel of fortune	Spin 1	Bad luck
	Spin 2	Fame
	Spin 3	There but for fortune
	Spin 4	The stranger
	Spin 5	Through the mist

You could create your own headings for the floors or spins.

PORTFOLIO FOR EXTENDED TASK ON DRAMATIC METAPHOR

You need to cover the following:

- your and the group's preparation, planning and shaping
- your contribution to the roles of deviser, designer, director and performer
- rehearsal process
- decisions you and the group made relating to audience, performance space and genre and style.

If this project was being done as a mock for the practical exam, following the preparation period you would have ten hours to create your performance and the portfolio. The portfolio is created as you go along and should represent about two and a half hours of work.

TOP TIPS

1 As an alternative to the ways of structuring outlined in this sub-section, follow the example of the Greeks on shaping and structuring a drama. Use the **unities of time, place** and **action** when you plan some of your dramas. The action all takes place on one day in the character's life and in one location. This simple structure has many advantages, besides the obvious one that you only have to create one set. Greater concentration is placed on developing character and the audience is not distracted from the character by changing locations and new information to take in. Characters spend longer on stage so you can get to know them and their concerns. This is particularly important if the genre is **tragedy**. You need time to empathise with a character if you are to take their plight seriously.

2 At the beginning of this sub-section it said that rules are there to be broken. Well, here comes the opposite of the tip above. Creating an extended plot is a very time-consuming and complicated process. In the time you have during your lessons you won't always be able to create long, well-ordered plots. This is where **montage**, **vignettes** and **collage** can be used to stitch longer dramas together without having to tie up all the loose ends, as you have to do with a well-constructed plot. This is working in a different way to that recommended using the unities of time, place and action. Montage, vignettes and collage gives you a way of switching scenes a bit like a film. The focus on character is reduced, but you can make the work visually exciting and cover great sweeps of content quickly and effectively. This is how you have worked on the tasks using dramatic metaphor on page 92.

3 Choose the structure which suits your content and your chosen genre, performance style and available time.

Practising for the written paper

(Instructions for answering these questions can be found on page 70.)

Section A

1 In the drama using the metaphor of the lift, outline the scenario as the character alighted at one of the floors. (When? Where? Who? Why? What? provides a simple structure for answering the question.)

   Note: the same question can be asked for a spin on the wheel of fortune, or pathway dramas.

2 Design a wheel of fortune for that drama. Create an annotated sketch which explains how it will be used in the drama.

3 Sketch out a plan for the 'pathway through life' drama. Label the key points in the character's life. Briefly outline the drama created at one of the points.

Section B

1 How did you explore, develop and shape the drama you created on the wheel of fortune stimulus? Include choices you made regarding structure, plot, genre, style of performance and conventions. Give reasons for the choices you made. (The same question can be applied to the 'lift' or 'pathway' dramas.)

2 Outline a plot you developed in your work on dramatic metaphor and set it out in scenes. Choose *one* of the scenes and explain in detail how it was shaped into a practical drama. (Where relevant, include examples of dialogue, monologues, sketches of settings, costume.)

3 Write an extended piece of dialogue for two or three of the characters from one of the scenes you created.

B4 Building belief – working with 'text' and taking a role

This project provides structures that can be applied to other content or texts you wish to use.

Covering assessment requirements of the course:

- There are several specific texts covered in this sub-section, enough to fill the requirements for coursework assessment Unit 1. The tasks also allow you cover both Macbeth and Romeo and Juliet as your full-length scripts, should you wish to do so. You can also refer back to any of this text work if you complete it before you do Unit 1, using knowledge gained to fulfil the requirement to study three scripts.

- It could likewise provide the basis for coursework assessment Unit 2, being used as the stimulus or theme for the Unit.

PROJECT SUMMARY

In this project you will work with a broad definition of 'text'.

Objective: To introduce ways of creating a role and exploring 'text'.

Purpose: To use structures for exploring and developing drama, which can then be used throughout your course on a range of 'texts'. Note: 'Text' is not only the scripts of published playwrights. The work you create in your improvisations can be turned into text, as can arrangements of selected or created visual images or movements; or selected or created artefacts or musical arrangements. Indeed, any prepared collection of materials or actions that seeks to communicate ideas can provide the springboard for creating text.

Specification coverage: You will be working with all the areas of study using 'text' as the starting point for the drama you create. There will be opportunities to consider the type of problems that need to be solved by designer, director, performer and deviser.

Portfolio: Tasks are included to develop your skills of reflection and help you create a working portfolio or the actual portfolios you need for the examination.

Information and exploratory tasks

When you prepare a drama and create roles or interpret a script, consider these aspects of your role to add quality and texture to your planning and performing:

- personality and attitude
- values
- status
- history
- power
- culture.

Personality and attitude

How does the particular personality or attitude of the role affect the drama? Are you working with a well-defined character with a clear personal history, attitudes and motivation? Or is it a type (representational acting), e.g. mother, policeman, tramp, business person? When you act a type you work with broad brushstrokes rather than needing lots of background detail. It assumes that all mother figures have certain common concerns and feelings. It is this aspect of character you work on, creating a general, universal mother rather than a specific one.

Exploration tasks, working in groups of 2–3 people

1 Create a **monologue** for a character with a particular personality trait and draw on observations you have made of actual people. Here are some possibilities:

  * a professional footballer/actor who has a giant ego speaking on a chat show
  * a teenager full of self-doubt and lacking in confidence talking to a year Head
  * a very sincere and earnest school teacher saying why they want to work at the school
  * a bubbly, vivacious person phoning a friend to ask them out
  * a computer fanatic who is very intense talking about their passion
  * an aggressive receptionist/telephonist answering an enquiry.

  Spend eight minutes devising the monologue.

2 Rehearse the monologue, one person acting, the others directing. Spend ten minutes on this. Then switch so the director gets to act and the actors direct.

3 Share the work with the rest of the group if you think this is helpful.

Status

This means the social standing of the character. A king or a beggar show the extremes, but between these two are many variations and complexities. In many societies throughout history, wealth has been a strong indicator of status, but there are exceptions. Even when he was a prisoner, Nelson Mandela had immense moral status.

Exploration tasks, working in groups of 5–8 people

1 Create a still image of the court of an emperor, which clearly shows four different states of importance in the hierarchy of the court. Spend three minutes on this. The whole class performs their work at the same time. See each individually if relevant.

2 Now find another way to show the four levels of importance. Again, take three minutes to do this. Repeat as many times as you think you can keep finding new solutions.

3 Do the same exercise as above for the following: a school playing field at lunchtime; the House of Commons at Prime Minister's question time; a main shopping street on a Saturday afternoon; a school staff-room. Work to a set timescale and make it short and sharp. Then run each of them one after the other to the beat of a drum or 'click' of a camera.

Power

What power does each character have in the drama? Someone with a gun in their hand might seem very powerful. Other forms of power are more subtle, e.g. knowing someone's weakness and sowing seeds of doubt in their mind, as Iago does with Othello, making him think his wife Desdemona is unfaithful to him.

Exploration tasks, working in groups of 4–6 people

1 Create five different still images or vignettes showing different forms of power. Spend ten minutes on this.

2 Now enact them, everyone performing at the same time.

3 Now find another two ways: five minutes to do this. Repeat as many times as you think relevant.

Values

What is the moral code of the characters? What is it they believe in and by what principles do they live their lives? This is the crux of the play *A Man for All Seasons* by Robert Bolt. The play hinges on Thomas More's refusal to sanction the divorce of Henry VIII.

Exploration task, working as a whole class

1 Read with your teacher, as a whole class, the extract below from *A Man for All Seasons*. The extract comes from near the end of the play, when More's family visit him in jail to try to persuade him to swallow his principles and so save his life. The historical setting doesn't make the scene any less relevant or emotional than if it were set today. It is a modern example of the **well-made play** (see pages 14 and 17) and relies on good writing to set up marvellous emotive acting opportunities for each of the three principal characters. The characters Jailer and Roper are supporting, with functional roles.

From *A Man for All Seasons* by Robert Bolt

Morning, cold grey light. Jailer lets Margaret, Alice and Will Roper into the cell. (The opening of the scene has them all greeting and making strained small talk. Then they come to the point.)

MORE:	*(looks at them, puzzled)* Well.
ROPER:	Sir, come out! Swear to the Act! Take the oath and come out!
MORE:	Is this why they let you come?
ROPER:	Yes … Meg's under oath to persuade you.

5	MORE:	(*coldly*) That was silly, Meg. How did you come to do that?
	MARGARET:	I wanted to!
	MORE:	You want me to swear the Act of Succession?
	MARGARET:	'God more regards the thoughts of the heart than the words of the mouth' or so you've always told me.
10	MORE:	Yes.
	MARGARET:	Then say the words of the oath and in your heart think otherwise.
	MORE:	What is an oath then but words we say to God?
	MARGARET:	That's very neat.
	MORE:	Do you mean it isn't true?
15	MARGARET:	No, it's true.
	MORE:	Then it's a poor argument to call it 'neat', Meg. When a man takes an oath, Meg, he's holding his own self in his own hands. Like water (*cups hands*) and if he opens his fingers *then* – he needn't hope to find himself again. Some men aren't capable of this, but I'd be loathe to think your father one of them.
20		
	MARGARET:	So should I …
	MORE:	Then —
	MARGARET:	There's something else I've been thinking.
	MORE:	Oh, Meg!
25	MARGARET:	In any state that was half good, you would be raised up high, not here, for what you've done already.
	MORE:	All right.
	MARGARET:	It's not your fault the State's three-quarters bad.
	MORE:	No.
30	MARGARET:	Then if you elect to suffer for it, you elect yourself a hero.
	MORE:	That's very neat. But look now … if we lived in a State where virtue was profitable, common sense would make us good, and greed would make us saintly. And we'd live like animals or angels in the happy land that *needs* no heroes. But since in fact we see that avarice, anger, envy, pride, sloth, lust and stupidity commonly profit far beyond humility, chastity, fortitude, justice and thought, and have to choose, to be human at all … why then perhaps we must stand fast a little – even at the risk of being heroes.
35		
	MARGARET:	(*emotional*) But in reason! Haven't you done as much as God can reasonably *want*?
40		
	MORE:	Well … finally … it isn't a matter of reason; finally it's a matter of love.
	ALICE:	(*hostile*) You're content then, to be shut up here with mice and rats when you might be home with us!
45	MORE:	(*flinching*) Content? If they'd open a crack that wide (*between finger and thumb*) I'd be through it. (*to Margaret*) Well, has Eve run out of apples?
	MARGARET:	I've not told you yet what the house is like, without you.
	MORE:	Don't, Meg.
50	MARGARET:	What we do in the evenings, now that you're not there.
	MORE:	Meg, have done!

	MARGARET:	We sit in the dark because we've no candles. And we've no talk because we're wondering what they're doing to you here.
	MORE:	The King's more merciful than you. He doesn't use the rack.
55		*Enter Jailer.*
	JAILER:	Two minutes to go, sir. I thought you'd like to know.
		More sends Roper after the Jailer to try and buy more time. (This short section of dialogue has been edited out.)
	MORE:	Now listen, you must leave the country. All of you must leave the
60		country.
	MARGARET:	And leave you here?
	MORE:	It makes no difference, Meg; they won't let you see me again. *(breathlessly, a prepared speech under pressure)* You must all go on the same day, but not on the same boat; different boats from
65		different ports —
	MARGARET:	After the trial, then.
	MORE:	There'll be no trial, they have no case. Do this for me I beseech you?
	MARGARET:	Yes.
70	MORE:	Alice?
		She turns her back.
		Alice, I command it!
	ALICE:	*(harshly)* Right!
	MORE:	*(looks into basket)* Oh, this is splendid; I know who packed this.
75	ALICE:	*(harshly)* I packed it.
	MORE:	Yes. *(Eats a morsel.)* You still make superlative custard, Alice.
	ALICE:	Do I?
	MORE:	That's a nice dress you have on.
	ALICE:	It's my cooking dress.
80	MORE:	It's very nice anyway. Nice colour.
	ALICE:	*(turns. Quietly)* By God, you think very little of me. *(mounting bitterness)* I know I'm a fool. But I'm no such fool as at this time to be lamenting for my dresses! Or to relish complimenting on my custard!
85	MORE:	*(regarding her with frozen attention. He nods once or twice.)* I am well rebuked. *(Holds out his hands.)* Al —!
	ALICE:	No! *(She remains where she is, glaring at him.)*
	MORE:	*(he is in great fear of her)* I am faint when I think of the worst that they may do to me. But worse than that would be to go, with
90		you not understanding why I go.
	ALICE:	I don't!
	MORE:	*(just hanging on to his self-possession)* Alice, if you can tell me that you understand, I think I can make a good death, if I have to.
	ALICE:	Your death's no 'good' to me!
95	MORE:	Alice, you must tell me that you understand!
	ALICE:	I don't! *(She throws it straight at his head.)* I don't believe this had to happen.

	MORE:	(*his face is drawn*) If you say that, Alice, I don't see how I'm to face it.
100	ALICE:	It's the truth!
	MORE:	(*gasping*) You're an honest woman.
	ALICE:	Much good may it do me! I'll tell you what I'm afraid of; that when you've gone, I shall hate you for it.
105	MORE:	(*turns from her: his face working*) Well, you mustn't, Alice, that's all.
		Swiftly she crosses the stage to him; he turns and they clasp each other fiercely.
		You mustn't, you—
	ALICE:	(*covers his mouth with her hand*) S-s-sh … As for understanding,
110		I understand you're the best man that I ever met or am likely to: and if you go – well God knows why I suppose – though as God's my witness God's kept deadly quiet about it! And if anyone wants my opinion of the King and his Council they've only to ask for it!
	MORE:	Why, it's a lion I married! A lion! A lion! (*He breaks away from her, his face shining.*)
115		

Development task

2 In working groups you are going to act out the scene. However, first try using a rehearsal technique Brecht used with his actors, outlined below. You will have to discipline yourself to follow the instructions exactly or the skills the exercise is designed to foster won't be developed. Performers have to be disciplined and try new ideas and ensure they don't reject an idea before they've tried it fully. In this case you do first, then reflect.

TOP TIPS

- Working in pairs, or threes if there is an odd number, choose a section of the text which has two characters speaking (three characters if there are three of you) and take a role each. The first actor in your chosen section *describes* in detail what actions and stage moves they are going to make before they say their opening line. Once they have done this they deliver the line, putting in the actions and stage moves they've described.
- The next actor in the scene does the same, describing the actions and stage moves before going on to combine this with their speech.
- This process continues speech by speech until you have completed the piece of text being rehearsed.
- Once you have been through the piece of text in this way, run the scene without stopping and without the description. The description is in your head and you put in all the actions as you speak the lines.
- Join with another group and show your rehearsed sections to each other. Switch to another group and repeat.

Discuss: Do you think there was anything about the scenes that made them different from presentations rehearsed in a more conventional way?

List three advantages to working in this way. Now list any disadvantages you think the system has.

TOP TIP

This system of rehearsing is good if you are going to develop a scene up to performance standard. I recommend candidates taking the practical exam at the end of the course use this system for the early stages of the rehearsal process.

Students using the system for the first time often say it's slow. However, when you think that you are **blocking** stage moves as you go and adding lots of detail, it is a very efficient way of starting rehearsals. The detail it can add to a scene is vital, and detail is a key factor that distinguishes the work of high achieving candidates. As an added bonus it helps some people learn their lines more quickly.

Try this system of rehearsing again in future performance projects.

Performance tasks

3 Rehearse and present the script extract of *A Man for All Seasons* to an audience. This can be done as a rehearsed reading if you haven't the time to learn the lines by heart.

4 If you are interested in doing more work on the play, ask your teacher to get a copy of the text. In the text you will find other powerful extracts you could perform. Make four to seven working groups and each take a different extract; you can run them in sequence to make a collage of key moments from the play. Choose extracts because it is not practical for you to present the complete play, it would require far too much time. Creating a collage or vignettes from a full-length play is a practical way of dealing with the requirement of the specification to study a full-length play. As with task 3, you could make it a rehearsed reading rather than learn lines by heart, or even improvise from the text.

History

This is an important part of the **When**, which has implications for your drama.

At a personal level every situation will be shaped by the past experiences of the participants. If you are working on a specific historical situation or script, you must consider the different attitudes and values that were the norm in those times. Parents sending their children to be evacuated in the Second World War were making the decision in very special circumstances; it's not exactly like it would be now. It is interesting for a present-day audience to think about the fact that parents were willing to send such young children away from home into the keeping of strangers. It gets the audience thinking and if you get them thinking, you engage them.

NOTE TO TEACHERS

A full-length play written for a youth theatre on this topic is Vacuees and a short script is to be found in the Evacuees drama resource book (see bibliography; Kempe & Holroyd, *Imaging* series).

When working with a historical theme, research may be necessary and this may make you decide you do not have sufficient information or the desire or the time to find out more about a particular stimulus. This is one advantage of using an already created script: someone else has done the research.

Devising task, working in groups of 4–6

1 Look at the script extract from *A Man for All Seasons* again and list the ways the author uses to create a sense of the historical time.

2 Devise through improvisation or write a new scene for *A Man for All Seasons,* keeping it in the same historical genre. For example, following on from the extract on page 100, create a scene where:

- the family make a last visit to More on the morning of his execution (they all know there is no longer any escape)

- the head of More the executed 'traitor' is placed on a spike on London Bridge: citizens gather to view the spectacle, what do they say to each other?

- news of the execution is taken to More's home village: how do the local people who have known him take the news? Remember the time the play is set in: the King is powerful and it can be dangerous to cross those who hold power. To be a member of the royal court brings wealth, but also risk and danger.

Culture

People's behaviour, understanding and attitudes are influenced by their cultural background. The differences can be extreme; the film *Dances with Wolves* explores the cultural divide between settlers and Native Americans. They can be more subtle; sub-cultures exist within any culture or society. They are defined by such factors as where you live, how you live, fashion, religion, politics etc.

Performance task, working as a whole class

1 Working with your teacher you could use a script on the website (www.heinemann.co.uk/secondary/drama/) *Hoka Hey*, which deals with the clash of two cultures, the settlers and Native Americans. It was written as a school play and is a historical/political play, siding with the Native Americans. You could use it as one of the three scripts you have to draw from for Unit 1 of your coursework or at some other point during the course.

Devising task, working as a whole class or in groups

2 Look at the photographs of the people and houses. This is a particular place
and a particular culture. Devise through improvisation or write a script that
explores an aspect of this culture. It could focus on a variety of themes: the
humour of the people; the economic circumstances; fears; aspirations; the
coming together of the community for a particular event or cause; the
changes taking place in the community.

Practise and develop your acting skills

The playwright and director Brecht advised his actors to observe with
reverence. This is encouraging actors to really look at people. Observe how they
do common everyday jobs, listen to how they talk together, and bring these
things into your drama. Accurate observation plus insight is a great source of
pleasure for an audience.

1 Observe someone doing a particular job or in a particular situation. It could be someone you know or a stranger. Here are some examples: shopping; laying the breakfast table; coping with a toddler in a supermarket; shaving; waiting in a long queue; teaching a class; reversing into another car.

2 Back in the classroom **demonstrate** what you have observed to the rest of the class. Add a **commentary** to explain it all, as it is not a mime exercise but storytelling. In your demonstration make sure your audience gets the points you are making, both physically and verbally. This means your style of presentation has to be very clear, maybe even exaggerated. Remember all drama and theatre has a degree of exaggeration, even so-called naturalism.

3 Working as a whole class, one of you teaches your 'act' to everyone else and lets them perform it back to you, all at the same time. Insist they get it right and keep them at it until they're really into the swing of it. You can take turns at this, using it as an acting warm-up over a period of weeks. It can be repeated using new observations and new subjects, for as long as it is useful and interesting. Call it 'the observation warm-up'.

Practising for the written paper

(Instructions for answering these questions can be found on page 70.)

Section A

1 Create a short character study for one of the characters in the *A Man for All Seasons* extract.
(Use the headings: personality; status/power; values; history; culture)

2 Write a monologue for one of the characters you created or played in this section of work. Give directions for the delivery of the speech.

3 Outline the plan for one of the scenes you devised which grew from the *A Man for All Seasons* stimulus. (What? Who? Why? Where? When?)

Section B

1 Design a setting for the *A Man for All Seasons* extract. Make a ground plan and use other relevant sketches and notes. Explain how the design will fulfil the needs of the scene.

2 a As a costume designer, describe briefly your overall concept (period, style and colour scheme) for the costumes in your drama.
   b Using detailed notes and sketches show how you would costume two of the characters from your drama. Give reasons for your choices.

3 You are hoping to direct the play *A Man for All Seasons*. Make a case to the theatre manager as to why it is relevant for a modern-day audience. Give the manager your ideas for the staging of the play and the type of audience you want to target.

B5 Staging – defining the performance space

This is an area of drama and text work that can be taken too much for granted by GCSE students. When working on scripted plays the location is usually clearly established and the creation of a workable set is tackled by most drama groups wishing to perform the play. However, in improvisations and preliminary script work it is often neglected. This is a mistake. Creating the **Where** helps raise the quality of your practical drama. It involves defining the space and creating the setting. This can involve actually creating a setting and adding lighting, which in a classroom context is not likely to be elaborate. However, it is perfectly valid to work in a minimalist way, using the resources of the performers and the imagination of the audience.

Working in a minimalist way relates to a particular style of theatre often called **poor theatre**. This way of working was made popular by a Polish practitioner Grotowski, who emphasised the skills of the performer in his work, rather than design for sets and costume. This way of working suits the way many of you will have to work in your schools. If you are interested, you can find out more about the work of Grotowski in his book *Poor Theatre*.

NOTE TO TEACHERS

Plays for Poor Theatre **work to these principles and are short texts suitable as examples of contrasting texts needed for Unit 2 coursework assessment (see bibliography).**

In all of your work you need to make the set in your mind

Make sketches and drawings of what the setting might be like: if your drama is set in a living room, list the type of decor found in this particular living room. This is all pre-text work and is a preparation for action, creating the context for the actors. This preparation for action gives background to character and can be as effective at doing this as the more commonly used hot-seating. It also informs plot.

The same principles apply to working with costume and properties. Sometimes you will be able to get them, but when you can't, pre-text work creating drawings or lists informs the acting and plot and adds to the quality of the action. Remember it is the detail that makes the difference between high and lower grade candidates.

TOP TIP

Before you start acting out a scene, whether improvised or from a script, each character makes a frozen image of their role. Then in turn, or all together, describe what your character is wearing.

The tasks that follow take you through this way of working. They are deliberately based on a well-known text that many of you will already be very familiar with (the text is slightly cut and runs scene 1 into scene 3). This is to encourage you to concentrate on extending your skills as a performer or director and to think about the area of design.

Macbeth by William Shakespeare

ACT ONE – Scene One

An open place.

Thunder and lightning. Enter three witches.

	FIRST WITCH:	When shall we three meet again,
		In thunder, lightning, or in rain?
	SECOND WITCH:	When the hurlyburly's done,
		When the battle's lost and won.
5	THIRD WITCH:	That will be ere the set of sun.
	FIRST WITCH:	Where the place?
	SECOND WITCH:	Upon the heath.
	THIRD WITCH:	There to meet with Macbeth.
	FIRST WITCH:	I Come, Graymalkin!
10	SECOND WITCH:	Paddock calls.
	THIRD WITCH:	Anon!
	ALL:	Fair is foul, and foul is fair;
		Hover through the fog and filthy air.

(ACT ONE – Scene Three)

	THIRD WITCH:	A drum, a drum!
15		Macbeth doth come.
	ALL:	The Weird Sisters, hand in hand,
		Posters of the sea and land,
		Thus do go about, about,
		Thrice to thine, and thrice to mine,
20		And thrice again, to make up nine.
		Peace, the charm's wound up.

Enter Macbeth and Banquo.

	MACBETH:	So foul and fair a day I have not seen.
	BANQUO:	What are these,
25		So wither'd, and so wild in their attire,
		That look not like th' inhabitants o' th' earth,
		And yet are on't? Live you, or are you aught
		That man may question?
	MACBETH:	Speak if you can. What are you?
30	FIRST WITCH:	All hail Macbeth, hail to thee, Thane of Glamis!
	SECOND WITCH:	All hail Macbeth, hail to thee, Thane of Cawdor!
	THIRD WITCH:	All hail Macbeth, that shalt be king hereafter!

	BANQUO:	Good sir, why do you start, and seem to fear
		Things that do sound so fair?
35		If you can look into the seeds of time,
		And say which grain will grow and which will not,
		Speak then to me, who neither beg nor fear
		Your favours nor your hate.
	FIRST WITCH:	Hail!
40	SECOND WITCH:	Hail!
	THIRD WITCH:	Hail!
	FIRST WITCH:	Lesser than Macbeth, and greater.
	SECOND WITCH:	Not so happy, yet much happier.
	THIRD WITCH:	Thou shalt get kings, though thou be none.
45		So all hail, Macbeth and Banquo!
	FIRST WITCH:	Banquo and Macbeth, all hail!
	MACBETH:	Stay, you imperfect speakers, tell me more.
		I know I am Thane of Glamis;
		But how of Cawdor? The Thane of Cawdor lives,
50		A prosperous gentleman; and to be king
		Stands not within the prospect of belief,
		No more than to be Cawdor. Say from whence
		You owe this strange intelligence, or why
		Upon this blasted heath you stop our way
55		With such prophetic greeting? Speak, I charge you.
		Witches vanish.
	BANQUO:	Whither are they vanish'd?
	MACBETH:	Into the air; and what seem'd corporal melted
		as breath into the wind.
60	MACBETH:	Your children shall be kings.
	BANQUO:	You shall be king.
	MACBETH:	And Thane of Cawdor too; went it not so?

Preparation tasks

Work in groups of four or five with a large sheet of sugar paper and coloured pens.

1 Using the opening scene of *Macbeth*, sketch or draw how you imagine the location. Make notes if it helps, but don't be afraid to make primitive drawings. Have some fun and remember how bold you used to be with your drawings when you were at primary school.

2 On another sheet of paper convert these ideas into a set design. You can only use a maximum of three items from the original drawing.

3 Each group presents their set design to the rest of the class. This is not just a verbal account, you must demonstrate where everything will be in the classroom or studio – that means you get on your feet and pace it all out on your stage, showing how it will work. You are doing pre-text work, thinking like designers.

Preparation tasks – variations

1 Setting (**Where**): a living room of a house in your community.

   Time (**When**): the present, mid-day Saturday.

   Make a drawing of the living room with its furnishing and decor (sometimes you might also make a ground plan – see page 30). Are there any hand props in the room and are some of these relevant to the specific time, Saturday mid-day? This is pre-text work, which helps you consider how status, power values, history and culture will influence the scene. It's no longer just any house but a specific house and already contains hints about the characters who live there. Any drama you do needs to take place somewhere and at some specific time. Detailed preparation will improve the quality of your acting.

   Making a sketch is another form of brainstorming, and drawing, rather than writing, changes the focus from character or plot to the physical environment or setting. You don't always have to start your planning of an improvisation with the characters. For a change, start with creating a location. This will inform the development of character, i.e. the type of person who lives there or who would find themselves in such a setting. This is helping develop your expertise in area of study 4, defining performance space. It is also good practice for working as a designer, which you can choose to do for your summative task of Unit 1 of your coursework assessment.

   It really does help you create quality improvisations, aiding the development of dialogue and plot and offering additional possibilities. For example, a family photograph is included as part of the design for the room, which leads to a moment when the performer picks up a photograph and recalls times past, cueing a **monologue** or **thoughts in the head**. Or the religious icon on the wall signals something about culture and values. Even though you may not always be able to actually create this setting, it has helped you think about the context and will inform your acting.

   You won't always do the drawing as a first step, sometimes you will do it after you've developed characters or done some exploratory improvisations. There is no fixed formula – mix and match to suit your purpose and the time you have.

2 Sometime during your course, at a time arranged with your teacher, working groups should select and arrange a specific collection of props, artefacts or costumes that create the starting point for a drama. You will not want too much, but you want enough to intrigue. Groups of you can take turns throughout the course to provide the starting stimulus. Your teacher can work with you to create a rota so you all have this opportunity. For candidates taking the written paper there can be questions which require you to think

about creating stimuli. You can elaborate this idea by including a character(s) to go with the collection. The character can be hot-seated.

Development tasks

There are three witches in the *Macbeth* scene. Nothing in the text distinguishes between them in any way or gives any clue to character. The context is more important than character in this case. What do you think those witches are like as people? Where do they live and what is their history?

Turn them into characters and tell their story. Perhaps it is a story of ordinary working women. Where does their knowledge come from? Use structures, genres and styles you have been introduced to in your course to create their story, their drama.

The same sort of task could be done for the Porter in *Macbeth*. He lets the visitors into the castle and the murder of King Duncan is discovered. His role in the play is to open the castle gate, be drunk and, hopefully, lewdly amusing. What is life like for him and the rest of the servants at the castle? There is a whole drama waiting to be explored here, *Life Downstairs at the Macbeths'*.

Discuss: Why are there so few working people portrayed in Shakespeare's plays, with those that there are often being comic caricatures?

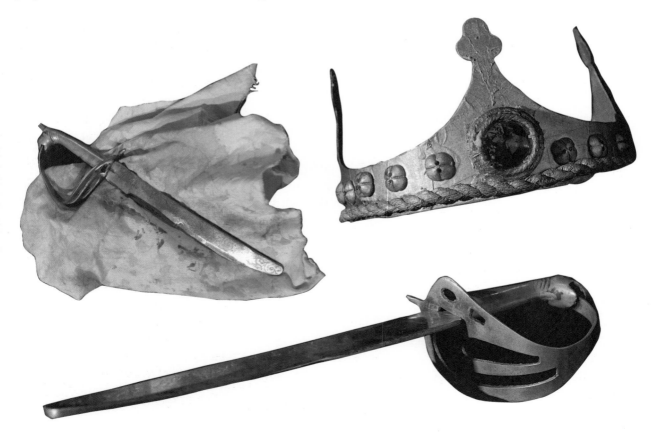

Extended performance task

This project can be used as the main focus for a twenty-hour coursework assessment Unit 1 or 2, or as the basis for a mock run for the practical exam (realisation test).

PROJECT SUMMARY

Objective: To create a ten- to fifteen-minute version of Macbeth.

Purpose: To work together as a whole class unit and in smaller groups to create a piece of theatre.

Specification coverage: You will be working with all the areas of study and you have the opportunity to work as deviser, designer, director and performer.

Portfolio: There are portfolio tasks to help you develop your drama expertise and your reflection and record-keeping skills.

Preparation tasks

Start by working together as a whole class to create a piece of ensemble theatre using the script extract on page 109. You can follow the same sequence of tasks used for *A Christmas Carol* on page 62–64, or adapt them to match your developing expertise and interests. For those who did work on *A Christmas Carol*, repetition helps you improve skills and regular ensemble work helps your drama class build team spirit.

Development and performance tasks

1 Two people play Macbeth and Banquo, everyone else represents the witches. Before you start, select your set design from the ideas you presented to each other in task 3 page 110 (if you haven't done this task, do it now). This gives you the starting point for the witches to emerge as if from the earth. The scene could start with a still image slowly coming to life, perhaps accompanied by music or percussion or a sound collage. This will get you all involved and thinking about the project.

2 As with *A Christmas Carol*, you could develop a selection of scenes to follow the ensemble opening scene. These could be small improvised **vignettes** or actual script extracts if you prefer. Remember script extracts will have to be short, as you only have a maximum of fifteen minutes for the whole play. The cutting of scripts is a good skill to develop, getting them down to the absolute basics. You can choose to play it straight as authentic tragedy, a melodrama or pastiche (see page 75), or update it to a gangster story or any other genre you think fits.

Some possible scenes:

SCENE 1
The witches

SCENE 2
The murder of Duncan

SCENE 3
The hiring of assassins and the murder of Banquo

SCENE 4
The banquet and the ghost of Banquo

SCENE 5
Lady Macbeth sleepwalking

SCENE 6
More predictions from the apparitions

SCENE 7
Birnham Wood comes to high Dunsinane. The death of Macbeth

A prologue and/or epilogue could be composed for the piece.

A further development would be to select an audience and rehearse and organise a performance of the play. This would cover area of study 3, audience.

[See page 131 in section B6 – *The Interactive Museum Project*, for another structure for working with *Macbeth*, or indeed any other text.]

PORTFOLIO TASKS

The tasks below should be selected in consultation with your teacher. Together you can decide which areas of expertise you need to develop and which could be used for either a working portfolio or one of your coursework portfolios.

Candidates taking the written paper can use them as preparation for the exam. Questions 1–6 are typical of Section A of the paper, and questions 7–9 are typical of Section B instructions for answering these questions can be found on page 70.

1 Write up or tape a dialogue or monologue which you created or delivered for the performance.

2 What genre did you use for the performance? List three ways in which your play worked with this genre.

3 List one point which you think highlights the most successful parts of your work on this project. Explain why it was successful.

4 Sketch or describe the setting you would create for a studio performance of the opening scene of *Macbeth*, the three witches on the moor.

5 Outline the background history you created for one of the witches in *Macbeth*.

6 What location would you use for a scene between two or three of the *Macbeth* servants on the night of the visit of King Duncan to Macbeth's castle? Sketch and/or describe the setting. (Remember it has to be a workable drama set.)

7 Working with a very limited budget, create practical costume designs for your production. Consider when is it to be set, characters' status and whether the actors play more than one part. Include body design and make-up if relevant.

8 Design a setting for your play that allows the action to flow from scene to scene with minimal interruption. Draw a ground plan, and with sketches and notes explain your ideas for the set. Include lighting ideas where relevant.

9 List two things you think you need to work at to develop your drama skills. Explain as fully as you can why you have listed these.

Staging and pre-text work on Romeo and Juliet

PROJECT SUMMARY

Objective: To explore a moment from Shakespeare's *Romeo and Juliet*, developing skills on pre-text and setting.

Purpose: To provide another opportunity to work with a new text and opportunities to apply conventions to text work.

Specification coverage: You will be using improvisation, drama conventions and the semiotics of theatre to create and perform a small piece of theatre. You will be working with the genre of tragedy. Conventions you will use: **hot-seating**; **thoughts in the head**; **alter ego**; **defining space**; and **preparing a role**. Performance style: **naturalism** (there could be a tendency to melodrama, it depends on how you play it).

Portfolio: There will be opportunities to develop your skills of reflection in a working portfolio or to create one of the coursework portfolios you are required to produce. For candidates taking the written paper there are some practice questions. Candidates not taking this option may also benefit from tackling these questions.

Context – What you need to know about the play

When: Set in the past in Verona, so there are different rules and beliefs governing the way people live their lives and behave. The historical and social context is not as today.

Character: Juliet is a fourteen-year-old girl.

She has a problem: Her parents have chosen an eligible young man for her to marry. His name is Paris and he is from a similar class to her own family. The wedding is to take place tomorrow. Unknown to her parents she is already secretly married to Romeo. It was a whirlwind romance, she has known Romeo only a matter of days. A trusted friar well known to her family conducted the service.

Just to complicate matters, Romeo is from a family hated by her own. And to make things doubly bad, in a recent street brawl between the young men of each family, Romeo killed her much-loved cousin, Tybalt.

What are her options?

- Confess everything to her parents.
- Kill herself.
- Use a potion given to her in a phial by the friar. The potion will slow her heartbeat down and for forty-two hours she will seem as if dead. At this time of year, and with infection rife in the city, she will be quickly placed in the family vault, alongside her recently slain cousin. The friar in the meantime will send a message to Romeo, who has been banished from Verona for killing Tybalt. The message will tell him to come secretly to the tomb and release Juliet. They can then build a new life far away from Verona.
- Any other options?

It sounds like a plot from *EastEnders*? Parts of the plot sound a bit far fetched and although it's a tragedy some aspects are almost melodramatic. Tragic acting often verges on the melodramatic – it can be a fine dividing line between the two.

Preparation tasks

Suggested group size: three to five people, or you can work as a whole-class group.

1 One of the group represents Juliet. She is in her bedchamber. Her mother has just left her, having presented her with the wedding veil from her own marriage. The wedding is to take place in the morning. Juliet almost rushed to the door to call her mother back and confess, but stopped herself. In her room she has the phial the friar gave her.

The rest of the group will do a mixture of **hot-seating** Juliet and taking on the role of her **alter-ego**. The group represent her inner thoughts, her parents' possible thoughts, her doubts, her questions, they make statements, give alternatives, etc. This is a variation on standard hot-seating, so Juliet answers or comments only as she thinks appropriate. Some of the comments will be statements, so no reply will be required. We are exploring the 'jumble of her mind' at this point in the play.

Once you have done your initial preparation and thinking (don't spend too long), improvise this without pause. You should be able to keep it going for an absolute minimum of three minutes.

2 Review.

- How did you create a sense of the historical and social context? On this first run through you may not have paid much attention to this. This is now your challenge, to recreate the hot seating/alter-ego in its historical and social context. Remember, the rules of behaviour and beliefs were different in those days. Ask your questions or make your comments as if you are from that time. Of course you can't be totally accurate, but when you work on the scene, try to consider how it might have been different in those times. This is part of being **drama intelligent**. Students who bring this type of intelligence to their work score highly in assessments.
- You need to capture the complexity of the situation. She loves Romeo, but she also loves her parents and they love her.

- Don't make it simple; complexity is interesting and Shakespeare was a complex playwright. Different points of view can 'battle it out' in one character – it's called **dialectical playwriting**, where opposite versions of the 'truth' are given a voice. In this case the character is arguing with themselves. You need to use the words you improvise carefully so they work in the context.

3 Repeat the hot-seating/alter-ego, working hard to make the scene as authentic and complex as you can. Try to capture the feel that it is from another time and culture.

4 Review again. Repeat as many times as you think necessary.

Development tasks

You have explored the state of mind of Juliet at this point in the play. The task is now to craft these thoughts into a piece of tragic theatre.

5 What hand properties and stage properties could be used to help the actress communicate to an audience? Remember you're selecting key properties that will enhance the performance. Make a list of possibilities, then select those you intend to use. Too many will cause clutter and reduce focus instead of heightening it. Some possibilities: a portrait of her parents; a crucifix; a ring; a wedding veil; a bed; a phial.

6 Define your acting space. Where is the door? Is there a balcony?

The key properties you have selected will be used in your drama, so you need to represent them. Remember they are for rehearsal, not a public performance. Scraps of material, a drawing or labels can be used to represent veils, dressing tables, bed etc. This helps the actor work in a naturalistic style by getting the setting fixed in their mind.

7 In groups or as individuals, create the properties you are going to use in representational form.

Performance task

8 Create a scene with Juliet in the bedchamber, the actors speaking her thoughts as she approaches their property or area of the room. Juliet uses the properties/setting as she feels appropriate. There is only one actor moving about the room as Juliet, the rest of the group contribute to her thoughts. The whole group is delivering the monologue.

You have all worked on the monologue as part of the devising process, but if you presented it in this way for the final performance, you'd be moving away from a naturalistic way of presentation. If the performance is to be strictly naturalistic, the actor playing Juliet will eventually deliver the whole speech alone.

9 Review the work created by considering the following questions. Does the use of properties help or hinder the actor? Does the language you have selected seem authentic and create the right tragic tone? **Adapt, edit,** make **additions**.

10 Rehearse and make it an exciting piece of theatre in the tragic genre. Your final version could be recorded, i.e. taped or written as a script, and used in your portfolio.

PORTFOLIO

- List any new ways of approaching text you used in this work.
- Which of these ways of working did you find interesting?

- Which ways of working would you use again?
- Did the work you did on staging and setting improve the quality of the drama produced?

Further developments

- Look at the monologue Shakespeare wrote for Juliet (Act Four Scene Three). How does it compare to your 'monologue'? Perform Shakespeare's speech, divide the lines between you, and create a group performance of Juliet, either in small groups or as a whole class.

- Create a **montage** of key moments from the play, moments leading up to the scene you've created and moments that follow it. These moments could be short snapshots or still images with captions that briefly come to life – **vignettes** or a **collage**.

- A whole-class play could be created. One actor delivers their Juliet monologue, other groups create the montage. Put it in order and you have a version of *Romeo and Juliet*. In this case, Juliet considering whether to take the potion has become the key, or defining, moment of the text. You could select an alternative defining moment.

- There is potential to create a ten- to fifteen-minute *Romeo and Juliet* as suggested for *Macbeth* on page 113. Look at the plan for *Macbeth* and see if you can apply a similar format to your version of *Romeo and Juliet*.

- Look at the improvised 'Romeo and Juliet Courtroom Drama' outlined on page 123. This enables you to create your own drama, devising a scene Shakespeare never got round to writing.

NOTE TO TEACHERS

West Side Story provides a contrasting text on the same story, useful for coursework Unit 1, which requires consideration of three contrasting texts. You are not introducing a totally new plot and it is a text that is very accessible, one that students can take short extracts from. The Jets and Sharks scenes go down well and the songs, such as When You're a Jet *and* America, *can be turned into dialogue or chants.*

Practising for the written paper

(Instructions for answering these questions can be found on page 70.)

Section A

1 Sketch or describe a specific property or artefact you used as a stimulus to start a drama. What possibilities for dramatic action or engagement did it offer?

2 Juliet is alone in her bedchamber considering whether she should take the potion. Write a monologue to show her state of mind at this point in the play.

3 *Romeo and Juliet* is to be updated and set in the present day. Design a graffiti name tag (Capulet or Montague) for one of the two 'gangs'. The name tag will be used as part of the set decoration and painted on a wall or fence.

Section B

1 Create a design for the Juliet bedchamber scene you worked on (page 116). Make a ground plan and use sketches and notes to illustrate your answer. Give reasons, showing how the choices you made will support the plot and theme of the play.

2 For one of the dramas you developed for performance, choose a suitable theatrical space for performing it. Consider the practical needs of your drama and draw a ground plan and create a set design to suit the needs of the presentation. Give reasons for the choices you make.

3 Explain your overall design concept for the drama you created, referring to each of the following as relevant: costume; make-up; lights; set design. Consider the practical needs of your drama and choose one of the design areas to give detailed examples of your ideas, e.g. costume design; make-up design; lighting design for a scene from the play; or a setting for the drama.

B6 Further ideas for dramatic action

Each format stands on its own, but can be linked to previous sections of the book. Many provide formats that can be applied to other content. This is particularly true of the suggestions which use aspects of the mantle of the expert structure.

Covering assessment requirements of the course:

- *Coursework Unit 1: the text extract from* The Trojan Women *and further ideas for work with* Romeo and Juliet. *There are also ideas which can link texts to devised drama, so the two elements complement each other.*

- *Coursework Unit 2: any of the following ideas could be used as the basis for the Unit. The ideas cover the requirement for stimulus, issue or theme based work.*

1 An alternative version of the Three Little Pigs

The original idea for this drama was the book *The True Story of The Three Little Pigs by* Jon Scieszka. *The Drama Classroom* (see bibliography) also has an adapted version of this story.

The Drama Classroom *gives a very good teaching sequence for this material, the learning area being stereotyping.*

Objective: To show how familiar material can be transformed into a new drama.
Purpose: Use very simple stories and plots as a starting point, which the drama group develop and transform into theatre to suit their purpose.

Specification coverage: This project gives the opportunity to use the skills and knowledge you have been developing in the course, to create a piece of practical drama. It could be the basis for Unit 2 coursework assessment, if it appeals.

Context

> Is anyone out there interested in a Fairy Tale miscarriage of justice? The case of the 'infamous' Big Bad Wolf. That's me, the Big – Bad – Wolf! That's not my real name of course, I was christened Winston Spencer Wolf by my doting parents. I had a
> 5   stable, normal wolf upbringing. I was lucky to be brought up without the trials and tribulations that can afflict so many youngsters these days. Dad was always in work so there was always food on the table and Mum was always there when I got home from wolf school.

10 We wolves have had to get used to being the outsiders in this world. Whenever they want a bad guy, who do central casting use? You've got it, the Big Bad Wolf. With stereotypical big fangs, slavering mouth, pointy ears and always wanting to gobble up someone's babies.

No wonder we tend to stick to our own kind, keep ourselves to ourselves. Believe me I've tried to integrate, but as my old Daddy
15 always said, 'You can't swim against the tide son, they've got their ways and we've got ours.' So how come I find myself in this prison cell? I didn't listen to Dad. I crossed the boundary, came over from the wrong side of the tracks into their cosy Fairy Tale world.

I sought help from a Little Pig who lived on the edge of town. I
20 thought of him as a neighbour and all I wanted was an adjustable spanner. His straw house was not very stable. A wolf would never have lived in such a ramshackle house. So when I knocked the door and it fell in right on top of him, is it my fault he has an asthma attack and chokes to death? And what do you expect a wolf to do
25 with a piece of fresh carrion?

At the second pig's house I had a sneezing fit and the stick house fell down. One of the beams killed him outright. Can you believe it, a stick house! I mean, what sort of schools do these pigs attend?

The third pig's house was in a better part of town and made of
30 bricks, obviously a better-connected pig. I rang the door bell and when they saw it was a wolf they began specially abusing me in the most insulting way. Well, I just flipped and gave back as good as I got. That's when the law arrived and I was taken to jail. The press and television got hold of the story and had a field day. You've
35 probably read the headlines. 'Wolf huffs and puffs and blows pig's house down'. I mean, let's be real, is that actually possible, even for a baby-eating monster? It's just not believable, but hey, I'm a big bad wolf. What chance have I got of justice?

Preparation tasks

You can plan your own preparation tasks (unless your teacher decides to do this with you) or you can follow the plan below. Select from the type of preparation tasks introduced in earlier projects. The purpose of these tasks is to explore the possibilities of the stimulus. You don't need to have decided where you are going with the stimulus, it can be very exploratory and 'messy' at this stage.

- In role as defence lawyers preparing this tricky case. How do you defend the wolf? Discuss the case with your client, the wolf.
- In role as the prosecution lawyers working out how you are going to attack the wolf's defence.
- Create characters who can be witnesses for the defence and prosecution, then let the lawyers interview them.
- Create character witnesses for the wolf, who know about the wolf's past.
- Create a series of still images showing how local pigs view the wolf and an alternative set showing how the wolf views himself.
- Still images could be created of past events, each incident having two images; one seen through the eyes of the pigs and another through the eyes of the wolf.

Possible plan of action:

1 Try the various tasks outlined above.

2 A whole-class role play getting ready for the trial. Lawyers prepare their briefs; interviews with witnesses; wolf worries; pigs want justice; judge powders his wig (just kidding!). This is using the mantle of the expert format, which mirrors the court case format suggested for 'The Romeo and Juliet court case' on page 123.

3 The trial.

4 The aftermath.

Development tasks

1 What is the underlying theme of the role play? By creating this pre-text what are you adding to the traditional story? What is it making you question?

2 Choose a genre and performance style that allows you to work with your chosen intention or that of the story on page 121.

3 Devise and rehearse.

Performance task

If you haven't already decided on an audience, do so now. Do you need to re-focus the work for this audience?

PORTFOLIO

Use ideas and information from earlier sections to create your portfolio.

Discuss: Are there other simple stories (they don't have to be fairy stories) that could be developed to make new dramas to pose questions about the world we live in.

2 The Romeo and Juliet court case – a contemporary version

PROJECT SUMMARY

Objective: To create a whole-class drama and explore who holds responsibility for the death of the two lovers.

Purpose: Opportunity for a whole-class drama activity, developing team spirit in the group using **mantle of the expert** format. An opportunity to work on pre-text, to weave your own drama from the original, generating an 'instant' text in action.

Specification coverage: The key focus is on area of study 5, improvisation, and working as devisers and performers.

Context

A young girl, Juliet, and a youth, Romeo, have committed suicide. Romeo knew Juliet's family would not approve of his marriage to their daughter. He went ahead and married Juliet in secret after a very short courtship. He was Juliet's first boyfriend. Up until his meeting with Juliet, Romeo had been seeing a girl called Rosaline. He knew Juliet's parents were organising another marriage for their daughter. He visited Juliet secretly.

A Court of Enquiry has been set up to establish who could be deemed to have had any responsibility for these tragic deaths. These people and their representatives will be called before the Court to answer for their actions. They will give their account and be cross-examined by the Court's team of investigators.

These are the people who could be considered to have had some responsibility for the suicides.

MRS. CAPULET: Encourages her young daughter to accept a marriage to an eligible young man, Peter Paris. Her daughter had shown no sign of being interested in marrying yet.

MR. CAPULET: Initially didn't think his daughter was old enough to marry, but allowed himself to be persuaded to consent to an arranged marriage. He considered Peter Paris to be very eligible. After the death of a cousin, Tybalt, in a street fracas, he decided to hold the wedding quickly, and make it a small family affair.

GOVERNESS: Took messages between Romeo and Juliet. She kept this secret from Juliet's parents. She knew Juliet was married to Romeo prior to the suicide, as Juliet had confided in her. Shortly after the secret marriage, the Governess was present at a row between Juliet and her father, when her father struck Juliet. Mrs Capulet was also present.

REVEREND
LAWRENCE: Knew Romeo well, had tutored him privately. Also knew he 'liked' the opposite sex. His last girlfriend before Juliet had been a young lady called Rosaline. The Reverend advised him not to get too carried away with romance and think about his future. Devised an elaborate plan for Romeo and Juliet to deceive Mr and Mrs Capulet and agreed to marry the couple. He hoped the marriage would help stop the bad feeling there has been between various families in his parish. He deceived Peter Paris, stringing him along that he would marry him to Juliet, when he knew she was already married.

MR MONTAGUE: Mr Montague had given his son a fairly free rein. His attitude was that young men sow their wild oats and then grow into their responsibilities.

Preparation

Roles:

- Each of those called before the Court has at least one representative, those of high status may have a team of representatives.
- The Court has chairperson(s) and a team of investigators.
- There may be character witnesses for some of those coming before the Court.
- There may be citizens who can add information.
- Court secretary – this could be played by your teacher.

You could include the ghosts of Mrs Montague, Paris, Romeo and Juliet. In the early stages of the drama only the 'audience' can see them and hear their comments, everyone else acts as if they're not there. Later they can challenge characters, who now hear and respond to them.

The opening speech the chairperson of the court might make:

> This Court of Enquiry has been called to find some meaning behind the tragic suicides of two young people. Two people with so much to live for. What does it tell us of the times we live in and the nature of our society? The bare facts of the case are well documented if somewhat confused: it was thought Juliet died from an overdose of a drug. The body was discovered the following morning by her governess. It has since emerged that Juliet was secretly married to Romeo. The Reverend Lawrence officiated at the marriage. He, I understand, met with Juliet the day before her suicide.
>
> Two days prior to the suicide, Mr and Mrs Capulet had announced the forthcoming marriage of their daughter to Peter Paris, the same Peter Paris whose stabbed body was found at the entrance to the Capulet vault. Then there is the violent suicide of Romeo and the stab wound in the corpse of Juliet. What are we to make of this? One can only assume at this stage that all these deaths are connected.

That young people, from such well-connected families, should take such a violent and desperate course of action fills me with sadness. Yet senseless and violent acts are becoming all too common on the streets of our city. It is time for us to reflect and perhaps start a process of healing. May this Court of Enquiry also become a Court of Reconciliation.

You can use this speech or you can devise your own to match the approach to the drama you are going to take. The speech above sets a particular tone for the work, it creates an atmosphere very different from a normal court of law and signals tragedy. The style of the writing could be very different. What you use or create will fix your genre and performance/improvisation style.

Development

The role play is set up (see diagram below for organisation of space). Everyone works in role preparing for the Court of Enquiry which is to take place in a few weeks' time (in real time, as opposed to drama time, it will take place in your next drama lesson).

Court Chairperson(s)	Ghost	Investigators
Mr and Mrs Capulet	Court Secretary	Mr Montague
Ghost		Reverend Lawrence
Peter Paris	Governess	other character witness

Representatives are helping their clients prepare the best response they can for the Court. Investigators and the chairpersons are making sure they have the appropriate procedure for the enquiry; after all, this is not a court of law. Witnesses are being consulted and decisions made as to who will be called and the order of appearance.

The Court secretary acts as an arranger of meetings between groups. Anyone wanting to have a meeting with another character or their representative or any of the other groups/individuals, must go through the secretary to arrange the meeting. The secretary will go to those people and see if they are willing to talk to you and find out when they can see you. People may try to shift blame, make alliances, apologise, get their story right etc.

The role play will last for one lesson. If you use the ghosts they can be observers and speak among themselves. At the end of the role play, they can add their commentary as to what they have witnessed.

Performance

The Court of Enquiry is set up as shown in the diagram below. The chairpersons and the investigators are responsible for the conduct of the Court, everyone takes their lead from them. Begin the role play and stay in role until the chairpersons retire to reach the pronouncement they are going to make on this tragic incident.

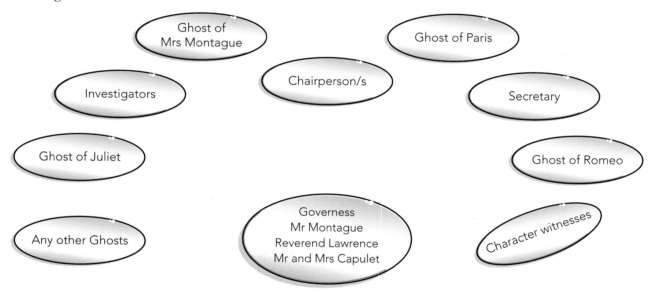

Chairpersons need to have a separate meeting supported by the investigating team to carefully draft a pronouncement on this tragic case. They have no power to punish, they can only draft words, which offer wisdom so that future generations may learn something from this tragedy.

While they meet, the other actors reflect on what they have been through, try to make their peace or become bitter etc. If you have used any ghosts – Mrs Montague, Paris, Romeo or Juliet – they can visit groups in turn to deliver their 'verdict from the grave'. You can now hear them and can answer them if you wish (you are using the theatrical convention of the ghost).

This two-session drama can stand alone as a piece of pre-text work on the play. You are working with issues raised by the play. You could take it further and generate your own drama/text from this work.

Possible developments

- How did the lives of those who played their part in this tragedy turn out? Create a montage of moments showing how life turned out for them. You can use still images, vignettes, monologue, diary etc.

- Romeo, Juliet, Mercutio, Tybalt, Peter Paris, Mrs Montague – all those who died – review the events and what has happened in Verona since their deaths. They do this from their position in heaven or hell. This is a theatrical ploy used by many playwrights, e.g. in *The Good Person of Setzuan* the gods view the deeds of the humans from on high and actually visit earth in disguise to mingle among the mortals.

- Artists meet with the leaders of the Verona City Council to talk about the creation of a statue, painting or some other artistic memorial, maybe even an annual play, which will remind the citizens and cause them to reflect. You will be working with the convention of **mantle of the expert**. Following the meeting the artists go to their offices and work in role on their designs and ideas. They will need to continually consult with the city leaders, either face to face or by phone and e-mail, if the scene is updated. The next stage is a meeting with the relatives (some of you now revert to your earlier roles in the court scene). Finally there is the public ceremony, with speeches, for the chosen work of art, whether it be the unveiling of a statue or the first night of a play.

- Any other ideas you wish to pursue.

Create your own dramas

The following starting points are for you to develop as you think best, using the knowledge and skills you have been developing on the course. Some possibilities are given, using formats and structures you have been introduced to in earlier parts of this book. However, it is now up to you to decide your **objective** and the **purpose** of the work.

> **TOP TIP**
>
> Choose starting points which cover areas of the specification you have not yet covered fully. This gives you a new challenge. To achieve at the highest levels it helps to set yourself challenges.

3 The House

Once this house was brand new. When something is new it carries such hopes, such potential. A new house, a new beginning. I wonder what those first occupants were like. I know the house was called 'The Pride of Eltwater'. All that is now gone. I know the house has been here a long time. Part of the landscape yet separate. It has seen good days and sad days, as most houses do. Yet this house reeks of memories. Oh, if only these walls could speak, what stories would we hear? Most locals avoid the house. Some, of course, cannot. Owners have come and gone, but of late none has lived there long. Yet I'm told it was once a house filled with laughter and joy. Carved into the great oak door frame is the word 'Eglantine'. What does it signify?

Preparation tasks

- Creating the setting: make a large drawing of the house; make a plan of the rooms on each floor of the house, label them; make a map of the surrounding area showing physical and human features.
- Look at the paragraph again and make a list of potential characters, both specific people (who will be given names) and roles (not named, but identified by jobs, e.g. a farmer).
- List or make still images of any drama moments suggested by the paragraph.
- Using one of the drama structuring formats you have been introduced to earlier in the book, plan a scenario (e.g. What? Who? Why? Where? When?).

Development tasks

- Create dramatic action, i.e. try the ideas out.
- Identify how you'd like to develop the drama, your intended audience, the genre and performance style to be used.
- Rehearse, edit, adapt and add.

Performance tasks

- Present the work.
- Review.

4 Backstage Drama

Context

Using one of the dramas or scripts you have performed, you are going to create a drama that shows what was going on backstage before and as the play was performed. This is a common theme in many dramas and has rich potential.

Research

- For an uplifting interpretation of the power and joy of being in a play, see the ending of *Our Country's Good* where the brutalised convicts are momentarily seduced by the sheer pleasure of putting on their play.

- Read the backstage scene in the play *Nicholas Nickleby*. It shows how the backstage drama can be effectively staged for theatrical excitement and comedy.

Preparation tasks

- Choose the drama that is going to be taking place out front and decide what everyone's role is. Who are the actors, who the stage crew, who the director etc.?
- Create a series of seven still images: one hour before curtain-up; thirty minutes before; fifteen minutes before; five minutes; three; one, you're on. Run through them rapidly, one after the other, and as each image is made, everyone speaks their **thoughts in the head**.
- Make still images of four key moments of the play onstage and extend the image to show what is going on backstage at the same time. Again, for each, give **thoughts in the head**. Turn each of the images (or some of them) into an improvisation, staying in role for each for a minimum of two minutes.

Development tasks

- Plan a piece of **sub-text** for two or three characters, i.e. something is happening between some of the characters that is nothing to do with putting on the play. Think of one example that is comic and another that is heart-rending. Act these out. Revisit one of the still images you created and when you bring it to life, everyone should enact one of their pieces of sub-text. If you had everyone involved in some sub-text in your final drama it could be overload. However, such a ploy is regularly used in plays and films for comic effect; **farce** is created by the convoluted comings and goings and lives of interconnected characters.
- Identify the type of drama you want to create or script. Decide on audience, genre and performance style.
- Rehearse, edit, adapt and add.

Performance tasks

- Present your performance.
- Review.

5 The Interactive Museum Drama

The format outlined here can be applied to any text or a historical theme. It works on the principle of creating pre-text, so although you won't be recreating a given text or historical period, you will use them as a basis for creating a new text. The beauty of this idea is that you can choose to use snippets of the actual text or devise around historical material if you want to. You can also recycle material you've already worked on, taking it in a new direction.

Context

An interactive museum of the type commonly found nowadays, where you move round and through a sequence of exhibits, looking at tableaux, listening to and watching tapes, pressing buttons, encountering actors, etc. to get a flavour of time and subject. Your drama task is to create such a museum. There are two examples given here using source material suggested earlier in the book. They illustrate how the format can work, but you could base your drama on a different play or subject. You can, of course, also adapt the format if you have better ideas.

Example 1 – The Macbeth Experience

Preparation tasks

• Create the recording you hear as you enter the museum. You can develop new skills and create a recording with suitable sound effects, or perform it live. It depends on the resources at your disposal and the time you are going to spend on the project. Below is an example you could use. It is written in a style gently satirising the 'Disney theme park' approach. If it is to be a more 'serious' museum, e.g. developed by the Royal Shakespeare Company or the Globe Theatre, you would write it in a different style. Later, try rewriting the speech below for one of these companies.

> *Taped voices of witches: (sound of storms, weird echoes etc.) Double, double toil and trouble, fire burn and cauldron bubble. A drum, a drum Macbeth doth come. (echoes of Macbeth, Macbeth etc.)*
>
> THE MUSEUM VOICE OVER: (*American accent*) Welcome to The Macbeth Experience. Step back in time a thousand years. The place is Scotland. A land divided into clans, each controlled by warrior lords, or thanes, as they called them, for example Macbeth and Banquo. When called upon by their King, they lead forth troops of soldiers to fight in the King's cause. That King is Duncan, King of Scotland. This is a hard land, a tough breed of people, a warrior race. Always the contest for power, the battle for land.
>
> The Macbeth Experience allows you to absorb the atmosphere of these times, to touch the play, to taste it. Follow your guide around the exhibits, try some detective work in the bedchamber and deduce how Duncan was murdered; meet one of the witches and the doctor who treated Lady Macbeth's troubled mind; try your hand at acting the ghost of Banqu ... o ... o ... o ... o ...
>
> *Taped voices of witches: Fair is foul and foul is fair, hover through the fog and filthy air. (Suitable sound effects added throughout the text.)*

- Make a list of the main exhibits you would have in the museum to tell the story of Macbeth. Then select five that absolutely must be there (six if you are to have six working groups).
- Make five or six working groups, each group focusing on a different exhibit. What artefacts, props or scenery would you include in your exhibit? Be selective, you're not actually creating an exhibit, but a drama representation, so a few key items will do the job. Note ideas and then select what you are going to use. Now create the exhibits in your working space. This may be quite rough and ready, e.g. drawings representing items and scenery, or you could do it in some detail. It will depend on the resources that your teacher can make available and the time you can spend on it. Consult with your teacher.
- Put some characters in the scene. Decide who they are and place them in position in sculpted poses. You now have a still image with scenery and props.

Development tasks

- In front of each exhibit there are two buttons for each character. Press one and they recite a monologue telling you about themselves at that point in the play. Press the other and the technology allows you to interact with them: you can ask them questions, hot-seat them. Spend some time practising this in your groups. When you are ready, create the five exhibits with the characters frozen within them. Those students who are not in the tableaux as characters, plus the teacher, walk round the museum trying the various buttons. Keep this going for as long as you think it sustains its purpose and interest.

- Back in your working groups, create a drama that is enacted when visitors enter your part of the museum. Sensors in the floor start the action as soon as visitors enter the room. When you are ready, the museum is created, but there are no visitors yet. Your teacher is the first visitor. As they walk to each exhibit, it comes to life.

- Some of you could take the role of guides, who could be used like workshop leaders to get visitors involved in the scenes. The visitors could be involved in **foruming** some of the scenes, replacing the actors and showing other ways of playing the scene. Their opinion can be asked, or question sheets devised for them to answer. In your groups, work out one way you are going to get the visitors to participate. Pair up with another group and take it in turn to try the ideas and get feedback.

Performance tasks

- This is a good way to create a participative piece of drama working in the **theatre-in-education genre**. Choose a group in your school to work with or a local primary school and take them through the 'Experience'.

Example 2 – The Evacuee Experience

This is done in exactly the same way as above. Below is an example of the opening recorded speech for this museum.

> Welcome to the 'Home Front'. This interactive museum depicts what it was like to be living in Britain during those momentous years 1939–45. The interactive, computerised displays will give you an insight, almost a taste, of what it was like to be alive during those eventful years. You may have grandparents or great grandparents who lived through these times, this is their story. We take you through that story from Neville Chamberlain's declaration of war broadcast to the nation on the wireless in 1939; into the phoney war as the nation waited for hostilities to commence; the introduction of rationing and evacuation; the London Blitz and battles on foreign fields; and finally the joy and spontaneous street parties, which broke out at the news of Victory in Europe in 1945. Join us in this experience and wonder at the achievement and resilience of our ancestors.

Discuss: What other plays or themes would suit being adapted in this way?

6 Script extract

Work with the short script extract below to develop your performing and directing confidence and expertise. This extract is a modern interpretation by Jean-Paul Sartre of the classic Greek tragedy *The Trojan Women*. The original was written by Euripides. Such short extracts can help you fulfil the specification requirement to study three contrasting scripts (coursework Unit 1). You are also working with a specific genre, Greek tragedy. If the extract grabs your interest you could develop it into a fuller drama, using formats suggested on pages 104 or 113.

NOTE TO TEACHERS

Short extracts can be used to give students an introduction into a variety of texts covering a range of genres. Use them regularly throughout the course.

Context

The Trojans have just seen their city destroyed by the victorious Greek army. Every male Trojan, man or child, is to be executed. Most have already been slaughtered. The women, both royal and humble, await their fate, to become the wives or slaves of their Greek conquerors. Talthybios, the messenger of the Greek army, comes to Andromeda, wife of the dead Trojan prince, and the hero Hector.

From *The Trojan Women* by Jean-Paul Sartre

Enter Talthybios with soldiers.

	TALTHYBIOS:	(*going to Andromeda*) Don't hate me.
	ANDROMEDA:	Why not?
	TALTHYBIOS:	I'm only the messenger.
		It is my distasteful duty
5		To tell you what my masters have decided.
	ANDROMEDA:	Come to the point.
		Don't be afraid to speak.
	TALTHYBIOS:	Your son.
10	ANDROMEDA:	Are they going to separate us?
	TALTHYBIOS:	In a way. Yes.
	ANDROMEDA:	We shan't have the same masters?
	TALTHYBIOS:	He won't have one at all.
	ANDROMEDA:	You're leaving him here?
15	TALTHYBIOS:	I don't know how to tell you.
	ANDROMEDA:	Spare me your scruples,
		Get on with your job, lackey.
	TALTHYBIOS:	They're going to kill him.
		Pause. She clasps her child to her,
20		*staring at him.*
		He continues quickly.

It was Ulysses who persuaded them.
He urged the Greek Assembly
Not to spare the life of the heir to the Trojan throne, because he
might sometime become the focal point of rebellion.
25   The Assembly accepted his resolution.
Pause
So it's no use holding on to him like that.
Give him to me.
30   *She resists.*
Come on now. Hand him over.
There is nothing else you can do.
Neither your city, nor your husband,
can protect you now:
35   neither exist any more.
Don't you understand, we give the orders now?
Do I have to tear him from you?
Don't be silly. Bow to the inevitable,
Accept it with dignity.
40   *Pause.*
For God's sake, isn't there anything
that can make you hand the child over?
Can't you see you won't gain anything
By trying my patience
45   Or making the soldiers angry?
If you do that, they'll just leave him to the vultures.
But if you hand him over quietly, we might even let you bury him,
and our generals will treat you with more consideration.
ANDROMEDA: (*to the soldiers*) Don't you dare lay hands on him!
50   I'll hand him over. Later.
They back away, watching her. She looks down at her child in
silence. Then slowly lifts up its hands one at a time, examining
the small fingers. She then holds one of its feet in her hands;
then runs her forefinger over the line of the child's mouth and
55   *eyes as though she had never seen the child, or any child, before.*
The soldiers approach her. She looks up. They stop. She walks
towards them holding out the child.
Here you are, take it: kill it.
Hit it with an axe. Throw it on a fire. It's yours.
60   I can't protect it: I could only give life to it.
What are you waiting for?
Take it.

TOP TIP

Use the Brecht 'description' rehearsal technique outlined on page 103 to rehearse the scene. The child is called Astynx and in reality was an infant. For theatrical purposes make it a baby, which can be created as a property.

7 Reflecting and creating a new drama

Devise the history of your drama group – creating a 'text' which reviews your time together and the progress you have made. This could be done near the end of your course, or you could do it yearly or even termly.

Context

An empty stage; the speech below is spoken, possibly by your teacher. Following it, the ghosts and shadows of past dramas appear, dramas both theatrical and personal! You are in charge of creating it.

> The audience awaits, and the air of expectancy is tangible.
>
> Upon this stage the stuff of dreams is made.
>
> The actors strain to touch your hearts or awaken your mind.
>
> To have you burn with anger at some injustice, then by turn make you howl with laughter at the foibles of human nature.
>
> This is the theatre!
>
> With its magical, dangerous attraction, drawing us to the shadows, that fret and strut their hour upon the stage and then are heard no more.
>
> Close your eyes!
>
> You can hear the echoes of long-lost performances that lived their lives here, upon this stage. The ghosts of this theatre's theatrical past.

Preparation

Select the ghosts you are going to resurrect and proceed to turn it into a practical drama.

Development

Edit, adapt, add and rehearse.

Performance

Video the final outcome. Each of you should add an individual commentary as to why you included your particular 'bits'. You have used practical drama to do an evaluation of some of your work to date.

Shorter practical reflection tasks

- When you complete any extended piece of drama work, make a visual collage of the successful moments. Add a caption to each moment. Record any results you think relevant.
- With a partner, take it in turns to create your individual best moments as a collage. Record them as above.

- Make a collage with captions of difficult moments. Use the record sheet on page 142 and in the spaces provided state how you would edit, adapt or add to improve the drama.

- Using video or audio tape, have someone take the role of interviewer on a radio or television show interviewing you about the project. They could use questions like those shown on the frame on page 144. You're making it a drama, so adapt the questions to suit the show. Try several different types of show. This is having a little fun with evaluation. However, you will find you still reach valuable and useful conclusions at the end of the process. List these once it's over and add them to the tape, speaking as yourself.

- Create a monologue of you giving yourself advice on how to improve your drama work or saying how wonderful you were. This is all a bit tongue in cheek. It's almost satirising yourself (see page 75), but remember: for satire to work it must have a strong basis in truth, so you'll have to be honest. All the best acting is honest.

8 Historical stimuli

Use historical background material to develop a drama – use the resource materials below as a starting point. Practise your skills of structuring and shaping. Decide on genre, performance style and audience. Those who wish to work with a script that deals with this issue could use *The Roses of Eyam* by Don Taylor.

I'm the one they all fear
Pestilence is my name
Plague and death is my game.
In and out I'll crawl and slither
Get all the City in a dither.
Once I'm here I spread
Pestilence is a name to dread.
First, they're fit and laughing
Then I'll catch 'em napping.
In fits and starts they'll jerk about,
Then they'll think it's only gout.
Sneezing next and fever too,
Stomach ache and boils, a few.
Swellings on their bodies they'll get
Until at last I'll close my net.
A ring o'roses their skin will show,
That'll be my final blow.
Sickness will have quickly spread,
Then my victims will be quite
DEAD.
(laughs)

Pestilence is my name

Plague symptoms

sneezing   aches and pains   headache   nausea   vomiting   desperate thirst
buboes (boils)   rash   black bruises   black tongue   Death

EXTRACTS FROM SAMUEL PEPYS' DIARY

7 June 1665	*This day much against my will, I did in Drury Lane see two or three houses marked with a red cross upon the doors, and 'Lord have mercy upon us', writ there – which was a sad sight to me, being the first of that kind that to my remembrance I saw.*
16 October 1665	*But Lord, how empty the City streets are, and melancholy, so many poor sick people in the streets, full of sores, and so many sad stories overheard as I walk, everybody talking of this man sick, and so many in this place, and so many in that. And they tell me that in Westminster there is never a physician, and but one apothecary left, all being dead.*

9 Updating a mystery play

Mystery plays were performed by ordinary working people. One of the cycle of plays regularly performed was *The Fall of Man*. It tells the story of Adam and Eve, how they are tempted and succumb to temptation. You could get your teacher to get a copy of the play or use the snippets below to set you off creating your own updated mystery play.

Read all about it: God creates world in seven days

Satan thrown out of heaven, sets up alternative kingdom to be called Hell

Sensation in Garden of Eden – serpent bites man

Adam blames Fall on Satan – God says take responsibility for your own actions

Fig leaves are going to be big in this year's summer collection

In this section you will find practical and factual information about the specification assessment. You can look at sections from the specification and read the explanation that tells you what is required.

1 The headings for this section are:
- Coursework – Unit 1 (includes useful analysis frames)
- Coursework – Unit 2
- Written examination paper (includes sample answers for sections A and B)
- Practical examination – preparation and realisation

Coursework – Unit 1

The specification states that two forms of evidence are needed for this unit:
- work in progress
- summative assessment.

Work in progress – using the portfolio

There is a choice as to how you present the evidence for work in progress. Portfolio evidence needs to be in one of the following forms:

> About 700 words of continuous prose

This is a bit like writing an essay. If you choose this method, you will need to keep notes of things you have done. You will then need to write an account of what you did and what you learnt. You must make sure that what you write meets the demands of the assessment criteria for this unit. They are printed for you at the end of section C – look at them and make sure that your account covers all of them.

> or
>
> Between 8 and 12 sides A4 or equivalent as a 'compendium', containing continuous writing, notes, diagrams, sketches, storyboards, scenarios, photographs, drawings, excerpts of dialogue, designs, character notes, views and ideas of self and others, as appropriate.

If you are organised, you can develop this method as your course progresses. Be careful, though. It is not like a 'project', where you keep just about everything and put it in a folder. What you keep must have meaning and show what work you have done. It is a good idea to develop your own shorthand system of noting where you have covered the areas of study. For example, the symbol 'AoS2' in the margin or on a diagram would indicate to the examiner that this was somewhere where you covered area of study 2. It would also help you keep an eye on making sure you cover all of the areas of study.

There does not need to be lots of writing. In fact, a lot of what you include could be notes and diagrams, photographs with explanations added, or short script extracts.

> **or**
>
> Between 6 and 8 minutes of normal size cassette sound tape, compact disc or standard VHS video tape commentary with written notes introducing the context and content.

This might seem a really attractive way of developing your portfolio, and if your school has the equipment and the editing facilities, it can be very successful with video. Do not underestimate the work involved. Easier to handle is using sound tape. There are lots of cassette recorders obtainable very cheaply, and popping a tape in and talking to it as you go along through the course can not only be a way of preparing evidence for your portfolio, but also a way of reminding yourself of what you have learnt. A good tip here is to start new tapes for new topics so as to make it easier to find things once they are recorded. Otherwise you could sit for hours trying to find them!

If you use sound or video tape, you must have a detailed contents page so that the examiner can find things easily, and know what is on the tape. You must also provide a short introduction, in writing, to explain what is on the tape and what you did. This does not need to be very long, but has to be there to satisfy the requirement for something in continuous writing.

> **or**
>
> A mixture of any of the above

It is of course possible to have a mixture of the above methods. There might be times when it is easier to have a record of what you did on tape, and to have notes and diagrams to support it.

> *You may find the forms on pages 142–148 helpful in keeping a record of what is going on in your work for your portfolio.*

Analysis and new action – A

These two sheets are to help you **analyse** and **review** the contribution you have made to the drama at each of the stages of the work in progress.

Date:

Task:

1 What is the **objective**, the **focus** or the **intention** of the drama?

2 How successful have I been so far in meeting the objective, focus or intention?

3 What ideas have I had to create new action?

Adaptation what we altered or changed in order to improve	
Editing what we cut out or decided not to include	
Additions what we added in order to improve the work	

4 Review your changes. Are you now meeting your objective, focus or intention more successfully?

- objective

- focus

- intention

5 Final overview of work you eventually created.

- What parts were you most pleased with?

- What was your strongest personal contribution to the work?

- Which aspects did you think needed developing further?

Questions to answer for a taped analysis

- What was our starting point in the lesson – what had the group achieved previously?

- What was good and what could be improved?

- What did the group or I decide to focus on in this lesson?

- Why?

- What did we adapt or change?

- Why?

- Were there any new ideas that we added?

- Why?

- Has the drama improved?
  - If 'yes', how is it better?
  - if 'no', why not?

- What still needs to be completed?

- What parts of our drama still need to be improved?

A writing frame for analysis

- Our play is about ...

- The good things in our play are ...

- The things that do not work are ...

- This lesson we wanted to improve our drama. To improve it we added/edited ...

- We did this because ...

- We also added/edited ...

- We did this because ...

- We adapted ...

- What we did was ...

- This improved the drama because ...

- At the end of the lesson the drama was better/worse because ...

- Next lesson we need to ...

Storyboard

Draw diagrams of your action in the boxes. Underneath write a short caption to explain what is happening.

Do this to show **significant** additions or adaptations.

Edit and add

Show what you have cut and what you have added. Use writing or diagrams or both. Explain your reasons.

Edited

Added

Analyse and reflect

Date:

Task:

Status: e.g. part of Unit 1 coursework

Stimulus/task/problem

Chart your individual contribution and thoughts, reflecting on the process you have followed, using the following headings.

1 Matching the drama to the original intention, saying how successful you were.

2 Ideas for new action:

   a adaptations? Why?

   b editing? Why?

   c additions? Why?

3 Review new action:

   a Are you matching the drama to the intention more clearly? Why?

   b If work is to continue, go back to 2 and repeat until the task is complete

Summative assessment

In a group of between three and six, you must be involved in a performance of either a section of one of the scripts studied, or a polished improvisation based closely on one of them.

In your group you must choose one of the following roles, and then carry out the task described for summative assessment in Unit 1.

Either

Deviser

Write a scene in the same style as one of the plays, with stage directions and character and staging notes. The scene should represent about 150 lines of dialogue, which will be performed by the group.

The scene should be complete and capable of standing on its own as a piece for performance. There must be more than two characters. Your notes on character and staging should give a prospective director enough information to understand what you, as deviser, intended and the sort of people the characters are. Stage directions should assume one way the scene might be staged. Look again at the section on page 48 about the importance stage directions can have and the use made of them (area of study 7). There should be a short statement identifying the genre you have chosen. You must also state:

- the name of the script you worked on
- what was chosen as the inspiration for your devising.

It is not enough to provide a scenario instead of a script. This is not sufficient to meet the requirements of this task, although it is likely that you will have prepared one as part of the devising process. It is permitted to provide a scenario as a context in which your scene is placed.

You may write an extra scene for one of the plays you have studied. If you choose to do this, make sure the dialogue is original, and that you consider introducing new characters created by you.

It may be that you change your mind about what you have written. Redrafting as a result of rehearsal may be submitted as part of your evidence, providing the original is available as well.

Or

Designer

You must prepare a design brief for one of the scripts studied. The script should be one from which the group has selected a section to perform or to develop a polished improvisation. The brief should be integrated and include ideas on:

- set
- costume
- make up
- lighting
- sound
- the use of masks (if appropriate).

You must provide evidence of a design concept that covers set, costume, make-up, lighting, sound, and any other design aspect you want to introduce, such as masks, dressing the set, props and furniture. You will need to take a view on the type of staging to be used.

You must include as part of your evidence the following as a minimum:

- an overall set design with ground plan and simple designer's sketch
- ideas (written or graphic) for the costumes, with at least one being in detail
- ideas (written or graphic) on make-up, with at least one being in detail
- an overall lighting design idea
- one lighting effect in the script selected
- one sound effect (or a reason for none).

Sketches and diagrams should be of a standard that enables easy communication. They should be clearly labelled, using or indicating colour where appropriate. Lighting and sound cue sheets should follow normal conventions. The final outcome should be seen as a set of ideas giving an overall, integrated design view of the play, which could be used at a first design meeting with a director

You will need to provide a short statement explaining how the design meets the intentions of the playwright, or if not, why; and reasons for the design you have decided upon.

Or

Director

Prepare director's notes for a section of one of the scripts or polished improvisation, with notes on characters and ideas on staging. This must be combined with actual direction of other candidates.

You must annotate an act, long scene or series of scenes representing about twelve pages of A5-size published script, or equivalent, showing ideas for character response, movement and blocking. Don't use someone else's set and staging, or the one provided in the edition of the play used; it is your responsibility to make decisions over the staging and set and style of performance, as it will influence other decisions. State this clearly.

Notes on character should indicate how you want the roles to be played, with a minimum of three characters described. Ideas on staging should include consideration of the type of venue to be used. Ideas on staging and style should be of sufficient clarity to enable a designer to start work on an initial design.

Or

Performer

Perform either a section from one of the scripts, or a polished improvisation based on one of them. You may do this in a group of three up to a maximum of six in number. Your group presentation should represent about three minutes' individual performance for each person as a maximum.

If you choose this option to perform you may also make contributions to the devising, design and direction of your performance.

The evidence of your work should include:

- exploration of the piece of script to be used
- use of improvisation and rehearsal as appropriate
- decision-making on style
- interpretation of the genre of the play
- interpretation of the intention of the playwright
- use of appropriate communication skills
- selection of the atmosphere to be created and the means of achieving it.

The performance itself should be appropriate to the work studied

Evidence will be primarily of the practical work you undertake. You may also use supporting material such as notes, sketches, diagrams and formal verbal presentations to the teacher or other members of the group, if you want to.

Work on the summative task should reflect the areas of study.

Coursework – Unit 2

In this section of the examination, your teacher will have selected a stimulus, issue or theme. What you have to do is devise and create a piece of drama leading from the stimulus, issue or theme that has been chosen. Each person in your group must have about three minutes of individual performance in the completed piece. You must work in a group of between three and six in number. The work for this Unit should represent about twenty hours of study.

What you have to do

- Research the stimulus, issue or theme.
- Decide on and investigate the cultural and historical context for your group's piece.
- Identify a genre. This must be different to the one you used in Unit 1.
- Decide on the intention of the piece, and the intended audience.
- Apply all of the areas of study to the devising, rehearsal and performance process. You should be used to this by the time you start this unit and should be able to use all the areas of study automatically.
- Apply knowledge, understanding and skills developed in Unit 1. It helps to refer back to work you have done and to things you feel you have learnt in the first unit.
- Using improvisation, explore possible outcomes. Do not go with the first thing you think of, or the most obvious. Also, be careful about modern-day 'issues' like smoking, drugs road safety, and the like. They can be very tricky to do well, and often stifle the imagination.
- Reflect on your own work and that of others, seeing how it influences or changes the work in progress. Remember the 'edit, adapt, add' process you were introduced to in Section B.
- Contribute ideas in the roles of deviser, designer, director and performer with regard to the developing drama and your own performance. Again, this should come automatically if you have been working through the exercises earlier in the book.

Evidence

As for Unit 1, evidence will take two forms:

- work in progress (Assessment Objective A, AOB, AOD)
- summative assessment (AOC).

Work in progress – using the portfolio

The evidence for work in progress will include:

- written work
- notes and diagrams
- discussion with other candidates and with the teacher
- practical activity, workshop and performance
- teacher commentary or notes.

Your evidence should reflect you and your group's response to the stimulus and the creation of the drama. It should demonstrate the application of each of the areas of study, and show that the roles of deviser, designer, director and performer have been used in the devising and rehearsal process. You must reflect on the work of others in your group, in other groups, or any other work you might have seen.

Keep your evidence for the work in progress in the form of a portfolio. The portfolio must show how you have contributed to the devising process, your thoughts and ideas on design and direction, and your views on the final performance of your role and the roles of others.

You must make sure you provide evidence to show you have considered each of the areas of study, including how the minimum demands have been met. You could do this by using each as a heading for evidence, although it is probable there will be overlap, and some might only need short responses indicating the decision taken and the reason.

Your portfolio evidence will be in the form of either:

> **About 700 words of continuous prose**

As for Unit 1, this is a bit like writing an essay. If you choose this method, you will need to keep notes of the ideas you have had and what you have done. You will then need to write an account of what you did, how it ended up, and what you learnt. You must make sure that what you write meets the demands of the assessment criteria for this unit. They are printed for you at the end of section C – look at them and make sure that your account covers all of them.

> **or**
>
> Between 8 and 12 sides A4 or equivalent as a 'compendium', containing continuous writing, notes, diagrams, sketches, storyboards, scenarios, photographs, drawings, excerpts of dialogue, designs, character notes, views and ideas of self and others, as appropriate.

Keep a record as your idea progresses and develops. Be careful, though. It is not like a 'project', where you keep just about everything and put it in a folder. What you keep must have meaning and show what work you have done. It is a good idea to use the 'What you have to do' list above as a checklist. As in Unit 1, you might want to develop your own shorthand system of noting where you have covered the areas of study. For example, the symbol 'AoS2' in the margin or on a diagram would indicate to the examiner that this was somewhere where you covered area of study 2. It would also help you keep an eye on making sure you cover all of the areas of study.

There does not need to be lots of writing. In fact, a lot of what you include could be notes and diagrams, photographs with explanations added, or short script extracts.

There must be a balance between having evidence for the final outcome, and having evidence for the research, development, exploration and polishing of ideas using drama skills.

> **or**
>
> Between 6 and 8 minutes of normal size cassette sound tape, compact disc or standard VHS video tape commentary with written notes introducing the context and content.

Video can be a very successful way of developing your portfolio, if your school has the equipment and the editing facilities. Do not underestimate the work involved. Easier to handle is using sound tape. There are lots of cassette recorders obtainable very cheaply, and popping a tape in and talking to it as you go along through the course can not only be a way of preparing evidence for your portfolio, but also a way of reminding yourself of what you have learnt. A good tip here is to use new tapes frequently, perhaps for new topics so as to make it easier to find things once they are recorded. Otherwise you, and the examiner, could sit for hours trying to find them!

If you use sound or video tape, you must have a detailed contents page so that the examiner can find things easily, and know what is on the tape. You must also provide a short introduction, in writing, to explain what is on the tape and what you did. This does not need to be very long, but has to be there to satisfy the requirement for something in continuous writing.

> **or**
>
> A mixture of any of the above.

The most comprehensive portfolios will contain a wide range of different ways of recording evidence of what you did and how you did it. Be aware of the best way to capture evidence. Sometimes a photograph can tell more than several pages of writing. Notes and sketches of development work, especially in the early stages, can demonstrate a lot of drama skills in action.

Summative assessment

In groups of between three and six, you will perform a piece devised and created by your group from the given stimulus, issue or theme. Each of the students in your group must contribute ideas in the roles of deviser, designer, and director, and you will all perform in the piece.

Your teachers will observe the process of devising, rehearsing and performance and will keep notes on evidence of what you do that meets assessment objectives, and the level of attainment you reach.

Remember that this is an examination. You must make sure that what you devise and then perform will show off your drama skills to the examiner. It is no good having an intense three-minute performance where you do not move or speak, for how can the examiner give you the credit for things if you do not do them?

In your preparation work make sure you use conventions to help polish the work.

Written examination paper

NOTE TO TEACHERS

The sample answers in this section are based on the exemplar question paper issued by OCR 2001. This paper used a stimulus item on Tutankhamun's tomb and the script The Roses of Eyam *by Don Taylor.*

The written paper is based on a piece of script and a stimulus item that you will see at the latest by the end of January of the year you are taking the exam. This means you have roughly a term to work with this material. You need to work with **both** the script and the stimulus item. It is probably best to divide the time equally between the two items.

TOP TIP

Draw up a timetable for dealing with the script and stimulus. Create deadlines and stick to them.

The specification states you must consider *the potential for performance, and applying the areas of study*. This means doing what you have been encouraged to do earlier in the book. Here is a reminder of the process you have been encouraged to use throughout Section B of this book.

- Preparation tasks ⎫
- Development tasks ⎬ these three stages cover your exploration, development, rehearsal and summative presentation/performance.
- Performance tasks ⎭

When creating your own dramas you have also been encouraged to engage in the following process:

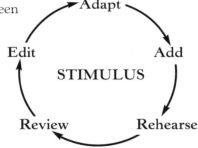

These are precisely the things you must do in your work with the examination stimulus. Look back over the book and select the preparation, development and performance tasks that suit your preferred way of working.

For work on the script there is a different emphasis, the sequence is:

These are things you need to cover as you explore the script. Select from the type of tasks you have been encouraged to use throughout this book.

TOP TIP

For both the stimulus and the script, make sure you create a summative performance. This should show that you have taken into account: genre; style of performance; chosen audience; definition of space; and design. If your performance covers all these factors, you will have done the essential background work to prepare yourself for the written paper. The summative performance will be work in progress, not a fully rehearsed performance for the public.

The question paper

The paper is divided into two parts, Section A and Section B, with an equal number of questions on both the script and the stimuli. You will not be able to answer *all* the questions by giving a straight account of what you did with the stimulus and script. The questions will require a mixture of the following.

- Direct accounts of work you did, plus reasons.
- Taking the ideas you had beyond what you actually did by explaining what you would have liked to do. Lack of time and working in a group sometimes stops you taking the drama where you would have liked to go.
- Answering on alternative approaches to the stimulus and script to those which you may have followed. The examiner can't set all the questions to match exactly how you did your drama: this is especially true with the stimulus. The knowledge and skills you have built up throughout the course will help you answer these questions.

Section A

In this section you have to answer six short questions, three on the script and three on the stimulus. There is no choice of question, you have to answer them all. You have one side of A4 and up to ten minutes for each answer. The time allowed and space allocated on the exam paper gives you an idea as to what is expected in terms of length and coverage for these answers. In Section A you *never* have to answer referring to the complete drama or script, only bits of them. The full drama/script or 'big picture', is covered in Section B of the paper. There will be ten marks available for each of these questions.

The answers can use:

- continuous prose (like an essay)
- storyboard
- notes
- diagrams
- drawings
- sketches
- dialogue excerpts
- plans
- plots (set out in scenes).

Which of the above you choose for your answer will depend on the particular question you are answering. For instance a question:

- on plot might involve a storyboard or a list of scenes
- may ask you to write a monologue or dialogue
- may require sketches of an artefact used as a property or stimulus for a drama
- may ask you to create a plan for an improvisation, for which you might use the format When? Where? Who? Why? and What? to answer
- on design might involve drawings or a ground plan
- on character study or performance ideas for the script might use lists.

(The above list also applies to Section B questions.)

TOP TIP

The important thing is to communicate your ideas to the examiner in the clearest, most straightforward way you can. Work in the way that suits your strengths. Some people will use diagrams, some prose, some storyboards. Throughout your course develop your favoured means of communicating for different types of question. Throughout Section B of the book there are sample questions for you to experiment with. Talk to your teacher and get feedback on which approach is most effective for you.

The sample question below comes from a practice paper your teacher has. The stimulus was based on the discovery of Tutankhamun's tomb by Howard Carter.

The tomb had four chambers, each with a ritual purpose. The east room was for rebirth, the south for eternal royalty, the west for departure towards the funeral destinies, and the north for reconstruction of the body.

sealed   sarcophagus

▼ East

sealed

◄ South   ▲ West

sealed

▶ North

passage

sealed entrance

stairs down

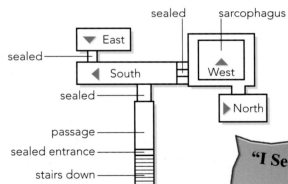

"I See Wonderful Things..."

Cautiously, the explorers edged their way along the narrow passage. They had no idea what lay ahead. They had already passed one sealed door; now they came to another. Using a heavy iron spike, Carter cut a small hole at eye-level so he could see (by flickering candlelight) into the next chamber. Eagerly, he peered into the gloomy darkness. Then he turned to Lord Carnarvon, his voice shaking with excitement:

"I see wonderful things ..." he said.

(from a newspaper account of the discovery of the tomb in 1922)

Question: Plan and write a monologue for a character created in your work on this stimulus. Give the background and your intentions in your plan.

Plan and intention

The scene is set in the Royal Burial Chamber of the pyramid. The tomb is about to be sealed, the high priest places the curse on any who dare to enter in future years. My intention is to create a sinister atmosphere, it's almost a parody of the horror genre, but I'm not trying to make it a spoof. The style of delivery is declamatory.

Monologue

The time has come to seal the Royal Chamber. Take your places and bow your heads to our departed master. (He raises his arms and declaims.) Hear this all you who may dare to enter this tomb. The tomb is sacred, protected by our Gods. Should any dare to violate this sacred tomb their soul will be weighed on the scales of judgement and be damned. Your punishment will be to wander in the land of lost souls for ever. No resting place, just endless toil and purgatory. You have been warned and the echoes of this curse will reverberate for all time, from age to age. (lowers arms) Seal the tomb. (They exit.)

Examiner's comments

- The candidate has made it clear what the purpose of the monologue is.
  It places the curse on any who enter the tomb and this obviously creates possibilities for later action in the drama.
- The candidate is making it serious, as they stated they would, although it is very clichéd as they also said it would be. Therefore the candidate is demonstrating control over their work, they know what they are doing and why.
- There is a sense of how it should be performed: declaimed and copying the horror genre.
- The writing matches their intention.

Candidate's score for this answer: full marks, 10.

The next example question also comes from the same practice paper, but is based on the script stimulus *The Roses of Eyam* by Don Taylor.

Question. Look at the opening scene between Mompesson and Saville (lines 1–117). What are the key contrasting characteristics of these two roles? How would you show these contrasts in performance?

MOMPESSON

He comes across as:

A bit arrogant (e.g. 'Lesser men have done it').

Not realistic, a bit of a dreamer ('The rector of God has no enemies, only sheep to be fed').

Sincere and committed ('I've waited ten years for this day' etc.).

Not experienced in the life of working people, having spent all his adult life so far studying books.

Keen to do a good job, but he's also ambitious and thinks he should have been given a better job. He's still going to work hard at this one.

Politically naïve regarding the effects of the Civil War on people's attitudes.

SAVILLE

Saville is used by the author to give the audience background facts, so he's a bit neutral, at times like a narrator.

Practical, understands working people and their attitude to God.

Understands people's emotions and he's clever in the ways of the world ('You'll be unpopular at first').

Fatherly, he's kind and wants to help, not put down Mompesson.

From these lists I'd show these contrasts. Mompesson's arrogance and different class shown by a clear well pronounced accent, tall straight stature, head raised as if conscious of his own appearance. Saville an easy posture comfortable with himself and a less affected accent. Mompesson showing keenness and energy regarding his mission. Saville more calm, but able to give straightforward advice and shoot from the hip. Mompesson always intense and serious, Saville more relaxed and able to see the funny side of things.

Examiner's comments

- Has identified contrasting characteristics.
- Gives evidence from text to support analysis
- Has given practical performance ideas to show the contrasts on stage.

Candidate's score for this answer: full marks, 10.

Section B

In this section there are four questions, two on the script and two on the stimulus. You have to answer two questions and can choose from any of the four in this section. For each question you have 30 minutes to answer. The examination answer booklet (this is where you write your answers) gives you four sides of A4 paper to use for your answers. However, additional sheets may be added should you need them. The time you have for each question gives you an indication of the length and coverage needed to score at the highest levels on these questions. In these questions you cannot be so specific about the number of A4 sheets you might be expected to fill. It will depend very much on factors such as the number and size of sketches/plans etc. used. There are 30 marks available for each of these questions.

The answers can use any of the means listed above for Section A. These longer answers do not require different knowledge or ways of answering. They provide the opportunity to answer in more detail and to explain why you made the choices you did. Questions will cover the following areas:

Statement of what you are trying to communicate or achieve in the drama or interpretation of the script.	Vital for any of the questions.
Structure of a drama: • for the stimulus, the plot outline; the way you craft a piece of drama so that it does what you want it to • for the script, an analysis of the playwright's structure.	Essential in any question asking how you **developed** the drama or **interpreted** the script.
Examples of the particular features of the genre and performance style used for communication. Extracts of monologues, dialogues or script, which illustrate communication, should be included.	Essential in any question which asks how you **presented** or **performed** the drama. Essential to questions on **development** where use of genre and performance style for communication are explored.
How you explored the script or stimulus – the ideas and thoughts that were important to the development of the drama. They don't have to be your own, they could be other group members' or the teachers'. Any conventions you used to develop the drama; key decisions that were made that fixed the direction you took or would take given more time.	Essential in any question on **exploration**, **development** or **rehearsal**.
List what you edited, adapted and added and give reasons for your choices.	Essential in any question dealing with **development** or **exploration**.
Design concept – how the overall design works, this includes all aspects, costume, setting, properties, lighting, make-up, seeing them as all linked and connected to each other. This does not mean you have to create detailed designs for each. You explain your concept, justify it and choose examples from one or two of the areas to illustrate how you are going to achieve this.	Essential in questions on **presentation** and **performance**.
Semiotics of drama and theatre – how your intentions or those of the playwright were communicated to an audience through: acting, scripting; design; proxemics; any other shaping.	Essential in any question dealing with **presentation** and **performance**. Essential in questions asking about **exploration** to cover relevant ideas tried and decisions made regarding semiotics.

Examiner tips and advice for Section B

- Always give reasons for any choices you have made. Top candidates know why they are making decisions and the likely effect those choices will have on the drama.

- Write using your practical experience from both the course and the examination stimuli. Design ideas that you have practically created and experienced in your normal working space are invariably of a higher standard than designs for spaces you have no experience of.

For questions on the stimulus item:

- Don't use an 'English story approach' to plot. You are not writing a story! Using the English approach encourages you write imaginatively and forget the practicalities of how this is going to work as a drama. High marks are awarded to answers which are clearly workable dramas. You can waste a lot of time and effort writing lengthy stories, but unless there is an explanation of how they are turned into drama, it will gain you no marks. There are more efficient ways of outlining a drama plot and structure.

The sample answer below is working with the Tutankhamun stimulus.

Plot and structuring

Scene 1: Narrator outlines the background to the drama. The archaeologist Howard Carter and his team have been working at this site for many months, there are rumours of a curse.

Two archaeologists enter and talk of the rumour of the legend they have heard from the local people.

Scene 2: Flashback to the burial of a pharaoh. Ritual burial where the priest places a curse on any who should enter the tomb.

Scene 3: A quick succession of still images, vignettes and news flashes showing the discovery of the tomb and the riches within. News flashes of the excitement being created round the world.

Scene 4: 'Egypt is in, it is the latest thing'. A satirical song sung by the fashion conscious young people of London, New York and Paris. Each city has its own verse.

Scene 5: Narrator announces it is now 1956.

News flash 1: Britain and France invade Egypt – Suez Crisis.

News flash 2: Nasser new leader of Egypt. Colonists kicked out!

Enter official delegation of Egyptians who present their case for the return of 'plundered treasures' currently kept in the British Museum. They speak directly to the audience as if they are the British authorities.

Two British museum curators enter and speak directly to the audience, stating that to return the artefacts would destroy their collection and scientific research.

Scene 6: An old man seated in a chair speaks of being at the opening of the tomb. He goes through one at a time all who were there that day and what happened to them. As he speaks their ghosts appear. All had unfortunate lives: only the old man survives with his memories.

The play closes with the song of the curse 'It'll get you in the end', a satirical skit on the horror genre.

Writing your plan in scenes helps communicate it as a practical drama. If the question was about how you **developed** or **explored** the stimulus, then record the decisions you made on the road to creating this plot and choosing the structure, as in the answer below.

Decisions on genre

We decided to mix the genres of documentary and satire to create our drama. We decided we couldn't do a real documentary play as it would involve too much research. Also this wasn't what grabbed our interest. The documentary material was used for the discovery of the tomb by Howard Carter and the excitement that this created around the world. Then time moves on and there are news flashes on the independence of Egypt from Britain. The satire was used in the songs and the argument for returning the artefacts to Egypt.

Performance style

This was very declamatory for the documentary bits and exaggerated for the satirical sections. We tried several different styles, trying to make it serious and tragic, then a horror spoof, but we didn't think we were going to be able to get a strong enough plot to carry these. So we decided to go for a revue type approach, as this would let us mix genres and performance styles. We chose styles we thought we could carry off and which would add energy to the performance.

For the 'Egypt is in, it's the latest thing' song we originally did it as a rap, but then our teacher played us some 1920s Charleston songs and music and we ended up doing it as 1920s flappers. For the 'I'll get you in the end' song we straight away hit on 'The Phantom of the Opera', Andrew Lloyd Webber style. We had done a pastiche of horror shows earlier in our course with our teacher, so we devised the song in the same style we'd been shown then.

Characters

There were no characters who went through the whole drama. The old man was the nearest we got to creating a character, but he was not fully developed. If the drama had told his story then his character could have been developed more, there could have been scenes with the ghosts of his past. Perhaps he could have stolen something from the tomb. However, this was not the line we followed, we created a collage of scenes, where there were representational types rather than characters – the government officials, news flashes. We also had a narrator and the singers doing a cabaret style act.

Themes and reasons for these choices

The decision was to have two themes going on. First, the idea of who do these treasures belong to, the British archaeologists or the people of Egypt? Second, the curse of the tomb. We decided to deal with Howard Carter's discovery of the tomb quickly, as it just creates the background and was not our theme. The documentary bits were to make a point about who has a right to these treasures. Our research on Egypt brought up the Suez Crisis, so our teacher suggested that was a good link into this debate – the new independent country wanting its treasure back. This is political, so we thought satire a good way of working on this. We didn't want it all being too serious, so we used the curse of the tomb story line. This is the obligatory moment, because you can't do a drama on Tutankhamun without the curse! We decided to have a mixture of serious for the ritual and the old man talking and spoof for the songs. We also wanted to have the chance to try various styles and genres, rather than stick to one.

Evaluation of the choices

It was a bit of a mixture, but in the time we had I don't think we could have created a tight plot, so using a revue approach and creating a collage worked well. We did raise the issue of taking treasures from their place of origin and whether that is right. The songs were good fun to devise and perform and they created an impact. The old man talking was not so successful. I don't think the script we created for him was strong enough. The script of the curse was very effective. *The argument of who has the right to the artefacts had potential for more work, we only raised the issue in our play.

* Note: the candidate could write an example of the script exactly like the monologue written for section A (see page 159).

If the question is about **presentation** or **performance** then there needs to be a section on the staging of the drama. In the example below, the candidate's answer keeps it simple to match the resources of the classroom.

Staging

We decided on a studio approach to match the revue feel to the script. We had a raised area upstage where the songs were performed as in a cabaret. The rest was performed on an open stage with no scenery. The newsflashes and arguments about who should look after the artefacts were delivered straight to the audience, it relied on good clear acting. The problem scene, as far as the staging was concerned, was the ritual burial. We did consider scrapping it. In the end we kept it and used a mixture of straw, rose and red coloured filters on our lights, to create a different atmosphere from the steel blue filters we used in the other scenes. This only partially solved the problem as we had no costume or props suitable. We used narration to set the scene and paint a picture for the audience. We got this idea from working on Chorus's speech from the opening of Shakespeare's Henry V. In this play, Chorus tells the audience they'll have to imagine the horses and thousands of soldiers, as they only have a few actors and props to create the illusion.

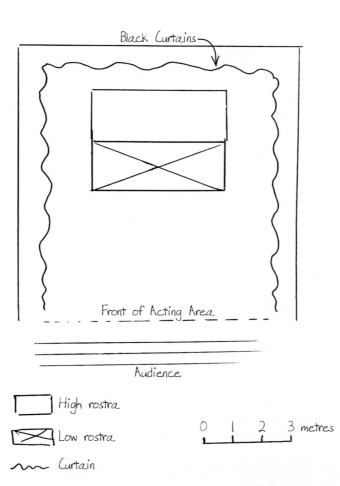

GROUND PLAN

Black Curtains

Front of Acting Area

Audience

☐ High rostra

☒ Low rostra

〰 Curtain

0 1 2 3 metres

Atmosphere

We also added a music background taken from the film 'Tomb' and added a chant in our own made-up language. The whole scene was acted in a stylised movement way, slow sharp moves and a lot of raised arms. At first it was a comic parody, but as we worked on it we decided to play it straight like they do in the Hammer horror movie 'The Curse of the Mummy's Tomb' clip we watched earlier in our course. We thought this would still be comic, but it ended up quite abstract and not a spoof at all. This is how we decided to keep it.

Costume

There was no attempt to costume authentically. Red t-shirts for the ritual burial, long Arab caftans for the Egyptians, a dark jacket and leg blanket for the old man and black T-shirts for everyone else.

The material above all relates to creating a practical working drama and reflects the quite short time you will have had to do the drama. Of course, drawings could be used, as could snippets of dialogue and song lyrics to illustrate the genre and style used. Note the following points.

- Everything is not complete and perfect, it is work in progress.
- You can use advice and ideas from others including your teacher. 'Copying' good ideas is a clever thing to do, Shakespeare did it.
- Reference is made to work and ideas from earlier in the course.
- Everything is practical, you can see how it would work in a school drama space.
- Design in this example is simple, representing what they could achieve in the time and with the resources available. Another candidate may have put a stronger emphasis on this. You must play to your strengths.

These same points would also apply to answers on script questions.

For questions on the script.

- The point is to bring to life the work and intentions of the playwright. To do this you must work like a detective and find out what the play's about. Is it a straightforward story or is there a sub-text with all sorts of themes and ideas being raised beneath the surface? Plays can have a whole subterranean underbelly to them.
- What is the genre of the script and is a particular performance style needed?
- Then probably most important of all, you need to work as a performer, director and designer to breathe life into those words. The text on the page must come to life and engage an audience.

TOP TIP

Never blame the script for dull work. Good directors, designers and performers can always make an engaging piece of drama. If the script doesn't come up to your standards you can add new text, working as devisers.

All the advice for Section B answers on the stimulus item apply to the text. You are using the same skills, there is nothing new to learn. Obviously, as the script is fixed, the questions don't put the same emphasis on devising, it is on **interpreting**, **communicating**, **rehearsing** and **performing**. The key point remains the same, you know what you are trying to do and you can do it.

The example below is part of an answer on *The Roses of Eyam* script, where the candidate explains their **design concept** for the play.

Design Concept

The play has both interior and exterior scenes and later in the play they change quite quickly, so I've decided not to attempt to create each scene naturalistically. My main concern is to keep the flow of action going, so any design must not slow the action too much. Therefore I've decided to create a composite set, which will remain throughout the play, with stage properties added as needed. These will be carried on by the actors in the new scene.

Upstage centre will be the village cross on a raised rostrum. The rostrum area will be large enough for actors to stand or sit on during the village square scenes. I'm not going to create any special area for the interiors, these will be created by change of lights with each family having their own fixed area of the stage and the actors carrying on a few stage props, e.g. a chair, or hand props, e.g. a bowl. The lighting for interior scenes will be straw coloured filters and for the exterior steel blue. Surrounding the acting area on three sides (not in front of the audience) will be six long thin boxes, they will be of the shape and size of coffins. The size will vary from full adult size down to the size for a small child. They will be painted a stone grey colour and placed on their ends so they look like standing stones. At various points in the play actors will move them and use them as coffins. They will always be returned to their original standing stone position at the end of the scene. Besides fitting in with the Derbyshire landscape, they symbolically represent the village cutting themselves off from the outside world.

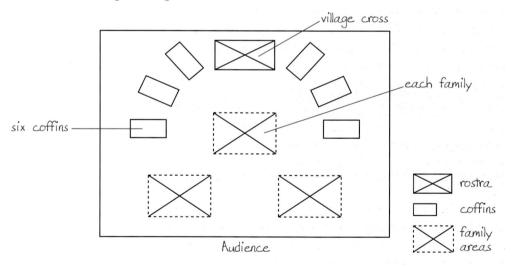

Costume

This will be symbolic rather than historically accurate (it wasn't practical for me to get historically accurate costumes). Slatey blue tunics and bottoms (to match the Derbyshire landscape). To this I'd add character items such as shawls for the villagers, neckpiece for Mompesson, white bonnet for Catherine.

As scenes change there will be traditional folk tunes played. I would prefer this to be live, using guitars and recorders, but it could be taped music.

Examiner's comments

- The material above gives an overall concept for the design of the production. This is how design needs to be viewed, rather than seeing it as a series of separate bits – costume, make-up, lighting, set. Running through a checklist of all the individual design elements, without any overall unifying concept, leads to poor answers. You fill a lot of space, but it is often uncoordinated and therefore doesn't get many marks. Note the following about the answer above:
  - the ideas are clear and practical, they would work
  - it is not only a crafted solution, but there are artistic ideas: the slatey blue colour to match the Derbyshire landscape; the standing stones to double as coffins and to symbolically represent the idea of the village cutting itself off from the outside world.
- The suggestions work with the theme of the play.
- The candidate may not have been able to actually create all the ideas, e.g. the standing stones/coffins or the slatey blue costumes, but the idea can be rewarded by the examiner. In rehearsal they could have used chairs to represent the coffins.

Candidate's score for section B answers: those illustrated here are all in the Accomplished Band, 25–30 marks.

Practical examination – preparation and realisation test

There are two parts to the final practical examination.

1 **Preparation:** Your starting point will be a piece of text and a stimulus, which will be provided by the examination board. You will be expected to consider the potential of both the text and the stimulus for performance. Choose which you'd like to develop into a performance piece (you may amalgamate them if you wish).

2 **Performance or realisation test:** You will have decided on your working group and created a plan of action. The final performance will be presented to the visiting examiner at a time arranged by your teacher.

Preparation – you can spend up to six weeks on this

The preparation involves experimenting as you have been doing in all the practical tasks throughout this book. The practical tasks in this book have used **preparation**, **exploration** and **development**. This is exactly the format to use to explore the text and stimulus for the practical exam. Use the experience you have gained in the use of: genre; style of performance; planning and structuring; semiotics; and defining the performance space to experiment with both script and stimulus. This will involve you thinking as deviser, designer, director and performer. It is working in the same way you have been using throughout the course. Now you are experienced and skilled in drama this is an opportunity to produce the very best work you are capable of for the practical exam.

Remember in your preparation work you need to consider all of the **areas of study** in relation to script and the stimulus.

The working process encouraged throughout this book has asked you to **edit**, **adapt**, **add**, **rehearse** and **review**. Continue to use this process.

Your teacher will be charting your progress, identifying your best work and recording it in their **teacher commentary**.

The question paper is in the form of a brief, which provides your starting point. The brief is based on the script extract and the stimulus item. This brief is responded to as part of the exploration and performance process, helping to make sure you cover everything you need to. The brief will ask you to consider the following points.

- Decide on your audience.
- What genre are you working in?
- What performance style are you going to use?
- Define the type of performance space to be used.
- How have the plays and themes you have explored influenced or affected your work?
- What is the link to the original starting points – the script and the stimulus?

You will also be asked to plan out how you will create your drama in the ten hours of the test and be reminded to include time for the portfolio. An example of a plan is given below.

Plan for Realisation

1 We selected the stimulus on Tutankhamun's tomb as content for our realisation.

2 Audience to be lower school, years 7 and 8. Studio performance space to be used.

3 Devising using the horror genre, but as a pastiche so it is a humorous look at this genre. From experiments in our preparation work we decided we could do a pastiche more effectively than a genuine horror.

4 Our performance style is to be over-the-top, melodramatic. However, not farcical, playing it straight and serious we think will make it funnier for the audience.

5 The setting is to be kept simple, using an open stage. New settings and atmospheres will be created by narration, change of lights and simple hand and stage props. One raised area to be used upstage centre.

6 The approach we are using is similar to plays by Michael Green, Plays for Coarse Actors. We are also drawing on improvisation work we did on pastiche and satire.

7 Our link to the stimulus is the idea of a curse on those who enter the tomb. This is our obligatory moment, you can't have a drama about an Egyptian tomb without the curse!

Due to time we have we decided to have a minimum number of scenes and focus on the following points.

1 What - those who enter the tomb have their lives changed forever.

2 Who - three archaeologists, the Egyptian, narrator, high priest, journalist, doctor, nurse. Cast will play more than one part each.

3 Why - purpose is to make a comic performance for years 7 and 8.

4 Where - tomb, the streets/journalists office, old people's home.

5 When - starts in the 1920s and then goes forward twenty years. Tomb scene set at midnight!

> **TOP TIP**
>
> Make sure you have done enough preparation to allow you to start your realisation straightaway when the ten-hour exam starts.

Checklist for the preparation process

- Carry out any relevant background research.
- Consider and explore the potential of the stimulus and script.
- Investigate, experiment with and establish resources which are practical and available for use in the realisation test.
- By the end of the preparation period you should have chosen what you want to base your realisation test on.
- Consider who you are going to work with and the best group size.

Your teachers will guide and advise your group on all of these issues to ensure you have the best chance of achieving a good result in the realisation test. Listen to their advice, as they have the experience to help you achieve your potential.

The realisation test involves creating a performance and portfolio. You have ten hours for the test.

Note: this does not include the time for the performance of the realisation for the examiner.

From your work in the **preparation** phase you will have selected either the script or the stimulus (or both) to create a performance in which each member of your group performs for the equivalent of a maximum of three minutes. A visiting examiner will come into your school to mark each individual's performance. The examiner will mark you on assessment objective C.

The examiner will also take away with them your **portfolio** and the **teacher commentary**, which will be used to mark you on assessment objective B.

> **TOP TIP**
>
> Before you start your test look with your teacher at the marking criteria for assessment objectives B and C, so you understand what the examiner and your teacher are looking for and how they give marks.

Work on your drama as you have been encouraged throughout this book. In the preparation phase you worked on **development tasks**; you will do so again only this time they will build towards the **performance tasks** and the final **realisation**. This is the process of creating and rehearsing the drama you are going to present to the examiner. Use what you have learned during the course and don't be afraid to copy ideas that have worked well. Use this book as a reference, drawing on ideas and ways of working you think are effective. Doing this is sensible as it uses the skills you have been developing.

Theatre is a craft and the realisation test is where you demonstrate your competence in the crafting of a performance. Everything you do does not have to be original, so don't burden yourself with that expectation. You can achieve maximum marks by breathing life into other people's ideas in an accomplished way.

You have to be realistic about the time you have for this performance. In ten hours what you produce will be very much work in progress – a polished improvisation. You will need to spend up to two and a half of the ten hours creating your portfolio. The portfolio should not be seen as something separate from the performance, but should be used to help you reflect on the quality and purpose of the drama. Again, look at strategies you have used throughout this book for developing a portfolio.

> **TOP TIP**
>
> Make the portfolio part of the process of creating a quality drama, use it to reflect on the developing drama as you work. Don't treat it as a 'mini project' to be done when everything is complete.

Checklist for the realisation test process

- Ten hours of supervised time.
- Create and perform a piece of drama in groups (normally between three and six), representing about three minutes of individual performance.
- Remember you don't get a group mark, but an individual mark, therefore it is important that each of your group has three minutes that shows their performance skills to best advantage.
- Use the skills of **deviser**, **designer** and **director** to create the drama and the skills of the **performer** to present it to the examiner.
- If you want to make a high quality drama and meet the assessment criteria for the exam, you must apply all the **areas of study** when creating and performing your work.
- Making sure you are covering all the areas of study is a form of quality check. You are working to the same system as the examiner and will demonstrate the skills they are looking for.

> **TOP TIP**
>
> If you work as an ensemble you get the opportunity to show a wide range of performance skills. A ten-minute performance could easily give all six in the group three minutes of performance each.

Portfolio requirements

You will prepare this during the ten hour session, and will present evidence of:

• preparation, planning and shaping (AoS 1 and 2)

• the application of the roles of deviser, designer, director, performer (AoS 7)

• rehearsal (AoS 5)

• decisions made with regard to AoS 3, 4 and 6.

Evidence should be in a permanent form. This evidence must include some writing. Make use of the proformas on pages 142–148. Examples of how the portfolio may be made up are:

About 600 words of continuous prose

or

Between 6 and 10 sides A4 or equivalent as a 'compendium', containing continuous writing, which may be notes or jottings, and any of the following as appropriate:

Scenarios	Sound tape recordings	Diagrams
Storyboards	Video tape recordings	Sketches
Writings		

or

Between 4 and 6 minutes of normal size cassette sound tape, compact disc or standard VHS video tape commentary with some accompanying explanation in continuous writing, which may be notes or jottings

or

A mixture of any of the above.

You have had practice at gathering evidence when you prepared portfolios in Units 1 and 2. Use that experience to make sure your documentation is a good record of what you have done. Make sure as well that it covers the areas of study and the four approaches: deviser, director, designer and performer. You can use any of the proformas on pages 142–148 if they are appropriate.

When you use sketches and diagrams, make sure they communicate their intention clearly, are labelled correctly, and use colour or an indication of colour where appropriate.

Examiner hints

➤ Focus hard on the project to ensure it is as good a piece of work as you can possibly create in the given time.

➤ You are working as a group so take your group responsibility seriously, don't waste anybody's time.

➤ Be realistic about what can be achieved in ten hours, don't spend too much time on elaborate resources.

➤ Decide what it is you are trying to achieve and create a drama that does this in a clear, straightforward way.

➤ Remember this is work in progress, a polished improvisation rather than full scale piece of theatre.

➤ Enjoy it and let your enthusiasm and commitment come across to the examiner.

➤ Remember this is an examination, so be conscious of the signals you are giving out to the visiting examiner. You will know about signalling from your work on semiotics.

➤ Produce Quality not Quantity.

Bibliography

Plays

Anon. *Everyman*. Nick Hern Books (1996)

Bawden, N. *Carrie's War* adapted by Staunton, R. Oxford (1997)

Bennett, A., Cook, P., Miller, J., Moore, D. and Frayn, M. (1961) *Beyond the Fringe*. Samuel French (1998)

Brecht, B. *Parables for the Theatre/The Good Woman of Setzuan/The Caucasian Chalk Circle*, trans. Bentley, E. Penguin (2001)

Brenton, H. (1980) *Plays for Poor Theatre*. Methuen

Cox, C, (1969) *Maria Marten, Murder in the Red Barn*. Samuel French

Edgar, D. (1980) *The Life and Adventures of Nicholas Nickleby, parts 1 and 2*. Josef Weinberger Plays

Green, M. (1978) *4 Plays for Coarse Actors*. Samuel French
   (1980) *The Coarse Acting Show 2*. Samuel French

Hall, P. (1985) *The Play of 'Animal Farm'*. Heinemann (1993)

Jarry, A. (1896) *Ubu Roi*. Methuen

Martin, B. (1983) *Vacuees*. From the *Act Now* series. Cambridge University Press

Odets, C. (1934) *Waiting for Lefty and other plays*. Grove Press (1993)

Sartre, J-P. (1969) *The Trojan Women*. Penguin

Shakespeare, W. (1605) *Macbeth*. Heinemann (1993)
   (1594) *Romeo and Juliet*. Heinemann (1993)

Sondheim, S. and Laurents, A. (1957) *West Side Story*. Heinemann (1993)

Soyinka, W. (2001) *King Baabu*. Methuen

Wertenbaker, T. (1988) *Our Country's Good*. Methuen

Plays for downloading from the website (www.heinemann.co.uk/secondary/drama/)

Art is a Weapon from *Worker's Theatre* (June 1931)

Cross, D. and Holt, D. (1977) *Hoka Hey*

Cross, D. with Knighton Fields Youth Theatre. (2000) *Jason and the Argonauts*

Tillotson, J. (1989) *A Christmas Carol*

Textbooks and novels

Ashwell, M. and Kempe, A. (2000) *Progression in Secondary Drama*. Heinemann

Aston, E and Savona, G (1999) *Theatre as Sign System*. Routledge

Booth, M (1991) *Theatre in the Victorian Age*. Cambridge University Press

Brooks, F. (1997) *Jason and the Argonauts*. Usborne

Bunyan, J. (1678) *Pilgrim's Progress*. Penguin

Grotowski, J. (1968) *Towards a Poor Theatre*. Simon and Schuster

Kempe, A. and Holroyd, R. (1994) *Imaging* (series). *Evacuees*. (student resource book). Hodder & Stoughton

Neelands, J. (1990) *Structuring Drama Work*. Cambridge University Press

Pavis, P. (1985) *Theatre Analysis: Some Questions and a Questionnaire*. New Theatre Quarterly 1(2) 208–212

Raphael, S., MacColl, E. and Cosgrove, S. (1985) *Theatres of the Left 1880–1935*. Routledge

Scieszka, J. (1989) *The True Story of the Three Little Pigs*. Viking Penguin

Swift, J. (1726) *Gulliver's Travels*. Oxford University Press (1998)

Taylor, P. (2000) *The Drama Classroom*. RoutledgeFalmer

Films and videos

Airplane (1980) Directors J. Abrahams and D. Zucker
Blazing Saddles (1974) Director M. Brooks
Dances with Wolves (1990) Director K. Costner
The Hustler (1961) Director R. Rossen
Jason and the Argonauts (film) (1963) Director Don Chaffey
Jason and the Argonauts (TV film) (2000) Director N. Willing
Young Frankenstein (1974) Director M. Brooks

Sound

Beyond the Fringe, EMI CDBTF61
Billy Bragg
Bob Dylan
Woody Guthrie
John Lennon
Ewan MacColl and Peggy Seeger